Electricity and Magnetism Science Fair Projects

Library of Congress Cataloging-in-Publication Data

Gardner, Robert, 1929–
  Electricity and magnetism science fair projects, revised and expanded using the scientific method /
by Robert Gardner.
      p. cm. — (Physics science projects using the scientific method)
  Includes bibliographical references and index.
  Summary: "Explains how to use the scientific method to conduct several science experiments about electricity
and magnetism. Includes ideas for science fair projects"—Provided by publisher.
  ISBN 978-0-7660-3418-1
  1. Electricity—Experiments—Juvenile literature. 2. Magnetism—Experiments—Juvenile literature.
3. Science projects—Juvenile literature. I. Title.
  QC533.G37 2010
  537.078—dc22
                          2009026548

Printed in the United States of America

092009 Lake Book Manufacturing, Inc., Melrose Park, IL

10 9 8 7 6 5 4 3 2 1

To Our Readers: We have done our best to make sure all Internet Addresses in this
book were active and appropriate when we went to press. However, the author and the
publisher have no control over and assume no liability for the material available on
those Internet sites or on other Web sites they may link to. Any comments or suggestions
can be sent by e-mail to comments@enslow.com or to the address on the back cover.

♻ Enslow Publishers, Inc. is committed to printing our books on recycled paper. The paper in
every book contains between 10% to 30% post-consumer waste (PCW). The cover board on the
outside of each book contains 100% PCW. Our goal is to do our part to help young people and
the environment too!

Illustration Credits: Tom LaBaff and Stephanie LaBaff

Editorial Revision: Lily Book Productions

Design: Oxygen Design

Photo Credits: Shutterstock, pp. 3, 6, 26, 44, 78, 118, 138; Wikimedia Commons, p. 98.

Cover Photos: © 2009 Jupiterimages Corporation (magnets); Shutterstock (hand).

Revised edition of *Electricity and Magnetism Science Fair Projects Using Batteries, Balloons,
and Other Hair-Raising Stuff,* copyright © 2004.

Electricity and Magnetism Science Fair Projects

Revised and Expanded
Using the Scientific Method

Robert Gardner

Enslow Publishers, Inc.
40 Industrial Road
Box 398
Berkeley Heights, NJ 07922
USA

http://www.enslow.com

Contents

Indicates activities appropriate for science fair projects.

INTRODUCTION

Electricity and Magnetism Science Fair Projects Using the Scientific Method

Physics is the part of science that deals with matter and energy. You and the world around you are made up of matter. All activity involves energy. By studying physics, you can unlock the secrets of matter and energy.

Electricity and magnetism are fundamental forms of energy. Try to imagine what your life would be like without electricity. Industrial and commercial work would be done in horse-and-buggy ways. There would be no television, computers, or CDs. You would be reading this book by candlelight.

The significance of magnetism is more elusive. However, by the time you finish this book, you will see that without magnetism, the electricity we take for granted would not exist.

◀ A boy's hand attracts electromagnetic energy through a glass.

Experiments and Projects

This book contains lots of fun experiments that show how electricity and magnetism work. You'll also be given suggestions for independent investigations that you can do yourself. Many of the experiments are followed by a section called Science Project Ideas. This section contains great ideas for your own science fair projects.

The experiments are all easy to do and safe to carry out when the instructions are followed as given. Consult with your school science teacher or some **other responsible adult** to obtain approval before starting any experiments of your own.

If any danger is involved in doing an experiment, it will be made known to you. In some cases, to avoid any danger to you, you'll be asked to work **with an adult**. Please do so. We do not want you to take any chances that could lead to an injury.

Most of the materials you'll need to carry out the projects and experiments described in this book can be found in your home. Several of the experiments may require items that you can buy from a supermarket, a hobby or toy shop, a hardware store, or one of the science supply companies listed in the appendix. As you begin to use this book, show it to one of the science teachers in your school. Perhaps the teacher will allow you and some of your friends to use the school's equipment. At times, you'll need a partner to help you. It would be best if you work with friends or adults who enjoy experimenting as much as you do. In that way you'll both enjoy what you're doing.

As you do these projects, you will find it useful to record your ideas, notes, data, and anything you can conclude from your experiments in a notebook. That way you can keep track of the information you gather and the conclusions you reach. It will also allow you to refer to other experiments you've done that may be useful to you in later projects.

How Scientists Search for Answers

When scientists have a question to answer, they start by researching. They read scientific literature and consult online science databases that are maintained by universities, research centers, or the government. There, they can study abstracts—summaries of reports—by scientists who have conducted experiments or done similar research in the field.

In this way, they find out whether other scientists have examined the same question or have tried to answer it by doing an experiment. Careful research will tell what kind of experiments, if any, have been done to try to answer the question.

Scientists do not want to repeat experiments that have known and accepted outcomes. Also, they want to avoid repeating any mistakes others may have made while doing similar experiments. If no one else has done scientific work that answers the question, scientists then do further research on how best to do the experiment.

While researching for the experiment, the scientist tries to guess—or predict—the possible results. This prediction is called a hypothesis.

The scientist hopes that a well-researched and carefully planned experiment will prove the hypothesis to be true. At times, however, the results of even the best-planned experiment can be far different from what the scientist expected. Yet even if the results indicate the hypothesis was not true, this does not mean the experiment was a failure. In fact, unexpected results can provide valuable information that leads to a different answer or to another, even better, experiment.

Using the Scientific Method in Experiments and Projects

The Scientific Method

A scientific experiment starts when someone wonders what would happen if certain conditions were set up and tested by following a specific process. For example, in an experiment testing the link between electricity and magnetism, you can ask the question: "How will a magnetic compass be affected by an electricity-carrying wire?" A guess about the answer is your hypothesis, and some possible hypotheses might be:

✓ The electrical current will not affect the compass needle.

✓ The electrical current will make the needle point in the same direction as the current is flowing in the wire.

✓ The current's magnetic field will control the compass needle in different ways, depending on the position of the compass.

Let's say the hypothesis is that the current's magnetic field will control the compass needle in different ways, depending on the position (placement) of the compass. You would then design an experiment to collect information to support or to refute the hypothesis.

A scientific experiment has only two variables—that is, only two things can change. For this experiment, one variable is the position of the compass (either above or below the wire), and the other variable is how the electrical current affects the needle.

The amount of electrical charge is not allowed to change, nor is the type of wire you use. If anything changed other than the placement of the compass in relation to the wire, then you could not be sure how a charged wire affects the compass needle.

Now, if your hypothesis turns out to be false, your experiment's results still provide important information. And those results can lead to further ideas that can be explored.

Scientists may develop logical explanations for the results of their experiments. These explanations, or theories, then must be tested by more experiments. If the resulting data from more experiments provide strong support for a certain theory, then that theory could be accepted by the world of science. But scientists are careful about accepting new theories. If the resulting data contradict a theory, then the theory must be discarded, altered, or retested. That is the scientific method.

Basic Steps in the Scientific Method

The best experiments and science projects usually follow the scientific method's basic steps:

- ✓ Ask questions about what would happen if certain conditions or events were set up and tested in an experiment.
- ✓ Do background research to investigate the subject of your questions until you have a main question.
- ✓ Construct a hypothesis—an answer to your question—that you can then test and investigate with an experiment.
- ✓ Design and conduct an experiment to test your hypothesis.

✓ Keep records, collecting data, and then analyze what you've recorded.

✓ Draw a conclusion based on the experiment and the data you've recorded.

✓ Write a report about your results.

Remember: To give your experiment or project every chance of success, prepare a hypothesis that is clear and brief. The simpler the hypothesis the better it is.

Your Hypothesis

Many experiments and science projects begin by asking whether something can be done or how it can be done. In this book's experiment, "The Minimum Ingredients for an Electric Cell," the question is: "What are the essential components of an electric cell?"

How do you search for the answer? For the hypothesis? You can first study the simple electric cell and learn about its early history. You will find out about electrolytes, a liquid or a damp solid through which electrical charges can move. Also, study about electrodes, material that conducts electrical current into or out of an electrolyte. Your study could suggest an educated guess to answer the question, a hypothesis: "To produce electricity, a cell needs two different types of electrodes and an electrolyte."

To test the hypothesis you will find out what methods, materials, and equipment are needed to design an experiment. You will learn what materials can serve as electrodes and electrolytes and then conduct experiments with them. For example, you can test whether electricity is produced when two electrodes made of the same material are used.

Designing the Experiment

Your experiment will be structured to investigate whether the hypothesis is true or false. The experiment is intended to test the hypothesis, not necessarily to prove that the hypothesis is right.

The results of a well-designed experiment are more valuable than the results of an experiment that is intentionally designed to give the answer you want. The conditions you set up in your experiment must be a fair test of your hypothesis. For example, in the experiment investigating the link between electricity and magnetism the magnetic compass you use must be kept away from objects that might attract it. Only the wire with the electric current can be allowed to influence the needle's movement.

By carefully carrying out your experiment you'll discover useful information that can be recorded as data. It's most important that the experiment's procedures and results are as accurate as possible. Design the experiment for observable, measurable results. And keep it simple, because the more complicated your experiment is, the more chance you have for error.

Also, if you have friends helping you with an experiment or project, make sure from the start that they'll take their tasks seriously.

Remember: Scientists around the world always use metric measurements in their experiments and projects, and so should you. Use metric liquid and dry measures and a Celsius thermometer.

Recording Data

Your hypothesis, procedure, data, and conclusions should be recorded immediately as you experiment, but do not keep this information on loose scraps of paper. Record your information in a notebook or logbook—one you use just for experiments. Your notebook should be bound so that you have a permanent record. The laboratory notebook is an essential part of all academic and scientific research.

Make sure to include the date, experiment number, and a brief description of how you collected the data. Write clearly. If you have to cross something out, do it with just a single line, then rewrite the correct information.

Repeat your experiment several times to be sure your results are consistent and your data are trustworthy. Do not try to interpret data as you go along. It is better first to record results accurately, then study them later.

You might even find that you want to replace your experiment's original question with a new one. For example, in the experiment asking the question, "Does an electric meter estimate conductivity?" you will test many solid objects, including cardboard, nails, plastic, pencils, pencil lead, silverware, wood, paper, coins, candle wax, chalk, glass, rubber bands, paper clips, aluminum foil, or a flashlight bulb. You will have to record the results carefully, and this might bring up another question: "Why is there a difference in how various materials conduct electricity?"

Writing the Science Fair Report

Communicate the results of your experiment by writing a clear report. Even the most successful experiment loses its value if the scientist cannot clearly tell what happened. Your report should describe how the experiment was designed and conducted and should state its precise results.

Following are the parts of a science fair report, in the order they should appear:

• The Title Page

The title of your experiment should be centered and near the top of the page. Your teacher will tell you what other information is needed, such as your name, grade, and the name of your science teacher.

• Table of Contents

On the report's second page, list the remaining parts of the report and their page numbers.

• Abstract

Give a brief overview of your experiment. In just a few sentences, tell the purpose of the experiment, what you did, and what you found out. Always write in plain, clear language.

• Introduction

State your hypothesis and explain how you came up with it. Discuss your experiment's main question and how your research led to the hypothesis. Tell what you hoped to achieve when you started the experiment.

• Experiment and Data

This is a detailed step-by-step explanation of how you organized and carried out the experiment. Explain what methods you followed and what materials and equipment you used.

State when the experiment was done (the date, perhaps the time of day, too) and under what conditions (in a laboratory, outside on a windy day, in cold or warm weather, etc.). Tell who was involved and what part they played in the experiment.

Include clearly labeled graphs and tables of data from the experiment as well as any photographs or drawings that help illustrate your work. Anyone who reads your report should be able to repeat the experiment just the way you did it. (Repeating an experiment is a good way to test whether the original results were obtained correctly.)

• Discussion

Explain your results and conclusions, perhaps comparing them with published scientific data you first read about in your research. Consider how the experiment's results relate to your hypothesis. Ask yourself: Do my results support or contradict my hypothesis? Then analyze the answer.

Would you do anything differently if you did this experiment again? State what you've learned as a result of the experiment.

Analyze how your tools and equipment did their tasks, and how well you and others used those tools. If you think the experiment could be done better if designed another way or if you've another hypothesis that might be tested, then include this in your discussion.

• Conclusion
Make a brief summary of your experiment's results. Include only information and data already stated in the report, and be sure not to bring in any new information.

• Acknowledgments
Give credit to everyone who helped you with the experiment. State the names of these individuals and briefly explain who they are and how they assisted you.

• References / Bibliography
List any books, magazines, journals, articles, Web sites, scientific databases, and interviews that were important to your research for the experiment.

Science Fairs

Some of the experiments in this book are followed by a section called Science Project Ideas. These ideas may be appropriate for a science fair. However, judges at science fairs do not reward projects or experiments that are simply copied from a book. For example, a diagram or model of an incandescent lightbulb would not impress judges; however, a series of experiments designed to test the longevity of lightbulb filaments made from different materials would gain serious consideration.

Science fair judges tend to reward creative thought and imagination. However, it is difficult to be creative or imaginative unless you are really interested in your project, so choose something that appeals to you. Consider, too, your own ability and the cost of materials needed for the project.

If you decide to use a project found in this book for a science fair, you will need to find ways to modify or extend it. This should not be difficult because as you do these projects you will think of new ideas for experiments. It is these new experiments that will make excellent science fair projects because they spring from your own mind and are interesting to you.

If you decide to enter a science fair and have never done so before, you should read some of the books listed in the further reading section. The references that deal specifically with science fairs will provide plenty of helpful hints and lots of useful information that will enable you to avoid the pitfalls that sometimes plague first-time entrants. You will learn how to prepare appealing reports that include charts and graphs, how to set up and display your work, how to present your project, and how to talk to judges and visitors.

Following are some suggestions to consider.

Some Tips for Success at a Science Fair

Science teachers and science fair judges have many different opinions on what makes a good science fair project or experiment. Here are the most important elements:

Originality of Concept is one of the most important things judges consider. Some judges believe that the best science fair projects answer a question that is not found in a science textbook.

Scientific Content is another main area of evaluation. How was science applied in the procedure? Are there sufficient data? Did you stick to your intended procedure and keep good records?

Thoroughness is next in importance. Was the experiment repeated as often as needed to test your hypothesis? Is your notebook complete, and are the data accurate? Does your research bibliography show you did enough library work?

Clarity in how you present your exhibit shows you had a good understanding of the subject you worked on. It's important that your exhibit clearly presents the results of your work.

Effective Process: Judges recognize that how skillfully you carry out a science fair project is usually more important than its results. A well-done project gives students the best understanding of what scientists actually do day-to-day.

Remember: Don't block your exhibit. Stand to the side when someone is looking at it.

Other points to consider when preparing for your science fair:

The Abstract: Write up a brief explanation of your project and make copies for visitors or judges who want to read it.

Knowledge: Be ready to answer questions from visitors and judges confidently. Know what is in your notebook and make some notes on index cards to remind you of important points.

Practice: Before the science fair begins, prepare a list of several questions you think you might be asked. Think about the answers and about how your display can help to support them. Have a friend or parent ask you questions and answer them out loud. Knowing your work thoroughly helps you feel more confident when you're asked about it.

Appearance: Dress and act in a way that shows you take your project seriously. Visitors and judges should get the impression that you're interested in the project and take pride in answering their questions about it.

Science projects about electricity and magnetism can include diagrams and charts showing the flow of current and the shape of magnetic fields. You can also photograph or draw the results of your experiments with electricity and magnetism. Illustrate any special tools and laboratory apparatus you set up. Be inventive about different ways of showing what took place. Record data from your observations in clear and easy-to-read charts or graphs. In this way your work and observations will be well displayed for the judges.

Safety First

Most of the projects included in this book are perfectly safe, but it's your responsibility to do them only as directed. Some experiments can be dangerous unless certain precautions are taken. The precautions necessary to prevent accidents and to make the experiments safe and enjoyable are easy to follow.

✔ Do any experiments or projects, whether from this book or of your own design, under the supervision of a science teacher or other **knowledgeable adult.**

✔ Read all instructions carefully before proceeding with a project. If you have questions, check with your supervisor before going any further.

✔ Maintain a serious attitude while conducting experiments. Fooling around can be dangerous to you and to others.

✔ Do not eat or drink while experimenting.

✔ Have a first-aid kit nearby while you are experimenting.

✔ Do not put your fingers or any object other than properly designed electrical connectors into electrical outlets.

✔ Never let water droplets come in contact with a hot lightbulb.

✔ When insulated wires need to be stripped, **always ask an adult to do it.**

✔Never experiment with household electricity except under the supervision of a **knowledgeable adult**.

✔The liquid in some thermometers is mercury. It is dangerous to touch mercury or to breathe mercury vapor, and such thermometers have been banned in many states. When doing these experiments, use only non-mercury thermometers, such as those filled with alcohol. If you have a mercury thermometer in the house, **ask an adult** if it can be taken to a local mercury thermometer exchange location.

And now, on to the experiments!

CHAPTER 1

Static Electricity: Charges at Rest

S ince ancient times, people have known a strange fact about amber. Amber—a brownish gold gem—is a fossil material made by trees. When rubbed with cloth, a piece of amber can attract and even lift light objects. In the sixteenth century, William Gilbert, an English scientist, demonstrated that substances other than amber had similar properties. Gilbert referred to materials that could attract light objects when rubbed as *electrics*. The word *electrics* comes from the Greek word for amber (*elektron*).

The experiments in this chapter are related to Gilbert's electrics. These experiments should be done when there is little humidity (damp air). Low humidity is most common in the winter because cold air cannot

◀For centuries scientists have known that the fossil amber, shown here held up to a light, becomes magnetic when rubbed with a cloth.

hold very much moisture. Your first experience with static electricity probably took place on a winter's day. You walked across a carpet wearing rubber-soled shoes. You reached for a metal door handle and *wham!* You felt a shock and perhaps saw a spark jump between your hand and the metal. Or perhaps you took off a sweater in a dark room and saw sparks moving between the sweater and your body. These experiences result from static electricity, the buildup of electric charges on the surface of materials such as wool and plastics. Unlike the electric charges that flow along wires, static charges are at rest.

In this chapter, you will find out how to create charges, discover ways to detect them, and investigate the different kinds of charges. In later chapters, you will find that these charges can move. Their motion can be controlled, and the energy they possess can be utilized. But you can begin by giving some objects a static charge.

EXPERIMENT 1.1

Getting Charged

Question:

Do electrically charged objects exert force on each other?

Hypothesis:

Yes, charged objects can attract or repel each other.

Materials:

- 2 rubber balloons
- 2 twist ties
- 2 strings about 30 cm (1 ft) long
- clear plastic tape
- door frame or table
- woolen cloth or paper towel
- 2 plastic rulers

- thread
- glass test tube or a glass rod
- various plastic objects, wooden pencils, balloons, and other objects
- silk, rayon, and nylon

Procedure:

1. Blow up two rubber balloons. Seal them shut with twist ties, and connect both to strings about 30 cm (1 ft) long.

Figure 1.

a)   b)

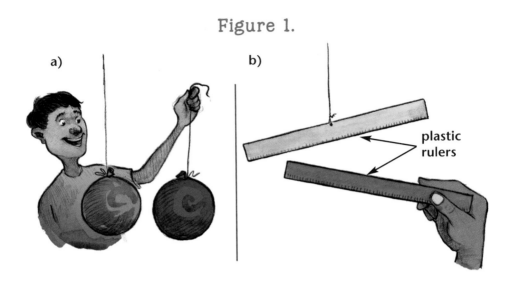

plastic rulers

a) Suspend a balloon with string. Then rub that balloon and a second with a woolen cloth or a paper towel. Bring the second balloon close to the suspended balloon. What happens?

b) Suspend a plastic ruler from a thread. Rub the ruler with a woolen cloth. Rub a second plastic ruler with a woolen cloth. What happens when you bring the second ruler near the suspended one?

2. Use tape to suspend one balloon from a door frame or table as shown in Figure 1a.

3. Rub this balloon thoroughly with a piece of woolen cloth or a paper towel. Then rub the second balloon in the same way.

4. Hold the second balloon by its string and slowly bring it near the suspended balloon. What happens? At what distance between the balloons can you detect a change? What happens as the distance between the balloons decreases?

5. Next, bring the piece of wool or the paper towel with which you rubbed the balloon near the suspended balloon. What happens? A similar experiment can be done using plastic rulers.

6. Suspend a plastic ruler by a thread as shown in Figure 1b.

7. Rub the ruler briskly with a woolen cloth. Rub a second plastic ruler with the same woolen cloth. Like the balloons, both rulers were charged in the same way; therefore, we might expect both rulers to have the same kind of charge. What do you predict will happen when you bring the second ruler close to the first one? Try it! Were you right?

What do you predict will happen when you bring the woolen cloth near the suspended ruler? Again, try it to see if your prediction was right.

Results and Conclusions

From your experiments with the charged balloons and rulers, you can see that charged objects exert a force on one another. When the charges on two objects are the same, do they attract or repel one another? How is the force related to the distance between the charged objects?

Procedure:

1. Once more, recharge the suspended ruler with a woolen cloth.

2. This time rub a glass test tube or a glass rod with the woolen cloth.

3. Then bring the glass near the charged suspended ruler. What happens this time? How can you tell that the charge on the glass is not the same as the charge on the ruler?

4. Repeat this experiment a number of times using different materials and different cloths. For example, try charging various plastic objects, wooden pencils, balloons, and other objects with silk, rayon, and nylon as well as woolen cloths and paper towels. Bring each charged object near the charged suspended ruler.

Results and Conclusions

What do you find? How many kinds of charge do there seem to be?

Here is a different way to charge objects.

Procedure:

1. Take two strips of clear plastic tape, each about 15 cm (6 in) long.

2. Fold a short length at each end of both strips to make a tab you can grasp. This will keep the tape from sticking to your fingers.

3. Place the sticky side of one strip on the nonsticky side of the other strip.

4. Next hold the strips by their tabs and pull them apart.

Results and Conclusions

What happens when you slowly bring the two strips near one another? How do the charges on the two strips compare? Are they the same or different? How can you tell?

Benjamin Franklin and Static Electricity

Benjamin Franklin was one of this country's founding fathers. He, like Thomas Jefferson, was involved in science as well as civic affairs. Franklin did experiments similar to those you have just done. He decided that there are two kinds of electric charge, which he called positive (+) and negative (−). He defined positive charge as the charge found on a glass rod rubbed with silk. He defined negative charge as the charge found on a rubber rod rubbed with fur. His experimental results led him to conclude that objects with the same charge repel one another; objects with different charges (one positive, one negative) attract each other. His definition of the sign (positive or negative) of the electric charge on an electrically charged object is still used by physicists today.

Based on the experiments you did, do you agree with Franklin's conclusion?

How do you think Franklin determined whether an object was positively or negatively charged?

 ## Science Project Ideas

- Suppose you add a third strip of sticky tape to two strips like those you put together in the last part of Experiment 1.1. (Place the sticky side of the third strip on the nonsticky side of the second.) How do the charges on each strip compare when you pull them apart one by one? Can you explain what you observe?

- Sprinkle some salt crystals on a dark sheet of paper. Hold a charged balloon above the crystals. Slowly lower the balloon toward the crystals. What happens? Can you explain what you observe?

EXPERIMENT 1.2

Inducing Charge

Question:

What is the force that causes electrical charges to move?

Hypothesis:

Like charges repel each other while opposite charges attract.

Materials:

- 2 balloons
- twist tie
- woolen cloth or paper towel
- wall
- a friend
- paper to tear up
- plastic ruler
- bubble wand
- bubble-making solution
- faucet

Procedure:

1. Blow up a balloon. Seal its neck with a twist tie.

2. Charge the balloon by rubbing it with a woolen cloth or a paper towel.

3. Place the balloon against a wall. It will stick to the wall.

4. Rub another balloon with a paper towel or woolen cloth. Then hold it above a friend's head. What happens to your friend's hair?

5. Tear a small piece of paper into tiny pieces. Then charge a plastic ruler by rubbing it with a woolen cloth or a paper towel.

6. Bring the charged ruler close to the bits of paper. What happens?

7. Dip a bubble wand in some bubble-making solution. Blow some bubbles.

8. As the bubbles fall, bring a charged plastic ruler near them. What happens?

9. Charge the ruler again. Then hold the ruler near a very thin stream of water flowing from a faucet. What happens to the stream of water?

Results and Conclusions

In the experiments you have just done, you did not charge the wall, your friend's hair, the bits of paper, the bubbles, or the water. Nevertheless, the charged balloon stuck to the wall, the other charged balloon attracted your friend's hair, the tiny pieces of paper were attracted to the ruler, and so was the thin stream of water.

The electrical attractions you saw can be explained by what is called induction. Suppose the balloon carried negative charge. When you placed it against the wall, negative charges in the wall were repelled and moved away from the balloon. They were *induced* to move away by the negative charges on the balloon. This left positive charges on the wall's surface, and you know that opposite charges attract. A similar thing happened when you brought the charged ruler near the bits of paper and the bubbles.

The stream of water was attracted to the ruler for a somewhat different reason. One side of a molecule of water has a slight negative charge, and the other side has a slight positive charge. Scientists call this a polar molecule. If the ruler carried negative charge, the positive sides of the water molecules were attracted to the ruler. The attractive force between the ruler and the molecules caused the stream to be pulled toward the ruler. Of course, the negative sides of the molecules were repelled by the ruler. However, the molecules turned so that the positive ends would be closer to the ruler. As you have seen, the force is less at greater distances. Therefore, the attractive force will be greater than the repelling force, causing the water to move toward the ruler.

⚡ EXPERIMENT 1.3

Detecting Charge: An Electroscope

Question:
What is the principle behind the simple electroscope?

Hypothesis:
Like charges repel and unlike charges attract, which make the electroscope's strips move apart.

Materials:

- **an adult**
- paper clip
- match or candle
- clear plastic cup
- scissors
- thin aluminum foil
- table or counter
- small nail
- clay
- plastic ruler
- woolen cloth or paper towel

An electroscope is an instrument that can be used to detect electric charge. It can also be used to determine whether an object is charged positively (+) or negatively (−).

You can build a simple electroscope using ordinary, inexpensive materials.

Procedure:

1. **Ask an adult** to make a hole through the bottom of a clear plastic cup. This can be done by heating the end of a partially opened paper clip with a match or candle flame as shown in Figure 2a. The hot paper clip can then be pushed through the bottom of the plastic cup.

2. While the paper clip is cooling, use scissors to prepare two small strips of aluminum foil. Each piece should be about 4 cm x 1 cm (1 ½ in by ⅜ in).

3. Use the cooled paper clip to make a hole near one end of each strip. Now open the paper clip so that it has a J shape.

4. Hold the paper clip inside the inverted cup. Push the long side of the paper clip through the hole in the bottom of the cup.

5. Slide the holes in the two aluminum strips over the bent end of the paper clip. (See Figure 2b.) The aluminum strips are called the leaves of the electroscope.

6. Set the inverted cup on a table or counter. Roll up a piece of aluminum foil into a small ball. Use a nail to make a hole in the aluminum ball. Then slide the hole in the ball onto the upper end of the paper clip, as shown in Figure 2c. Be sure the aluminum strips do not touch the table. Then seal the paper clip to the cup with a lump of clay, and your electroscope is ready for use.

7. Rub a plastic ruler with a woolen cloth or a paper towel. Slowly, bring the ruler near, but not touching, the aluminum ball. What happens to the two aluminum leaves?

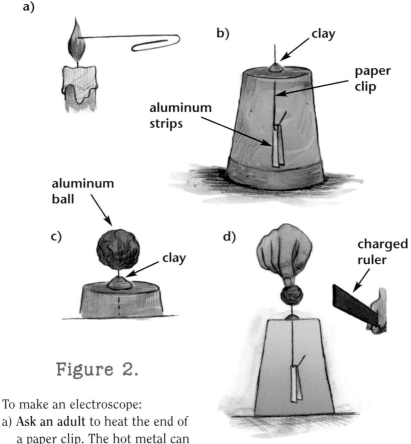

a)

b)   clay

aluminum
strips   paper
                                clip

aluminum
ball

c)   clay   d)   charged
                                                ruler

Figure 2.

To make an electroscope:
a) **Ask an adult** to heat the end of
   a paper clip. The hot metal can
   be used to make a hole in the bottom of a clear plastic cup.
b) Partially open the cooled paper clip. Extend the straight end through the hole
   in the cup. Add two small aluminum strips to the bent end of the paper clip.
c) Put an aluminum foil ball on the upper end of the paper clip. Seal the paper
   clip to the cup with clay.
d) What happens if you touch an electroscope, bring a charged object near
   (not touching) the electroscope, remove your finger, and then remove the
   charged object?

Results and Conclusions

Using what you know about induction, can you explain the behavior of

the leaves? How will the charge on the leaves compare with the charge on

the plastic ruler?

Procedure:

1. Next, charge the ruler again and hold it in one hand.

2. Before you bring the charged ruler near the electroscope, place a finger of your other hand on the aluminum ball at the top of the electroscope, as shown in Figure 2d.

3. Bring the ruler toward the top of the electroscope. Then remove your finger from the ball.

4. Next, move the ruler away from the ball. What happens to the leaves? Can you explain why?

5. Now, slowly bring the ruler toward the aluminum ball again. What happens to the leaves?

Results and Conclusions

What does this tell you about the charge on the leaves? Is the sign of the charge on the ruler the same or the opposite of that on the leaves? How do you know?

 Science Project Idea

- Investigate the various types of electroscopes. (They can be made in a variety of ways.) Draw diagrams to show how they are alike and how they differ.

EXPERIMENT 1.4

Some Static Effects

Question:

Can you easily demonstrate the effects of static electricity?

Hypothesis:

Yes. Static electricity charges can be created on many objects by simply rubbing their surfaces.

Materials:

- old pair of panty hose
- plastic bag
- plastic comb
- paper
- aluminum foil
- plastic wrap
- tape
- ping-pong ball
- plastic ruler
- paper towel
- flat piece of clear glass or rigid plastic
- 2 thin books
- woolen cloth or paper towel
- newspaper
- scissors

Figure 3.

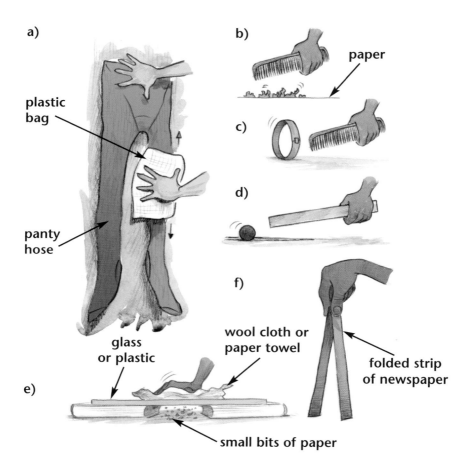

a)

plastic
bag

panty
hose

e)

b)

paper

c)

d)

f)

glass
or plastic

wool cloth or
paper towel

folded strip
of newspaper

small bits of paper

These experiments demonstrate static electric effects.

Procedure:

Following are a number of experiments that are like magic tricks. See
Figure 3.

a. Hold an old pair of panty hose against a wall. Rub the hose briskly
   with a plastic bag for a few seconds. Release the hose. Do they stick
   to the wall?

Remove the hose from the wall and hold them from the waistband. What do you notice about the shape of the hose?

b. Use a plastic comb to comb your hair. Then hold the comb near some tiny pieces of paper. What happens? Repeat the experiment using bits of aluminum foil and plastic wrap.

c. Cut a strip of paper about 10 cm (4 in) long and 3 cm (1 in) wide. Roll the paper into a narrow cylinder and tape the ends together. Lay the cylinder on its side so that it looks like a wheel.

Comb your hair with a plastic comb. What happens when you hold the comb near the paper wheel?

d. For a similar effect, place a ping-pong ball on a level surface. Rub a plastic ruler with a paper towel and hold it near the ball. What happens?

e. Tear a small sheet of paper into tiny pieces. Place them under a piece of clear glass or rigid plastic resting on two thin books. Rub the glass with a woolen cloth or paper towel. Watch the paper bits begin to dance.

f. Cut a long strip about 3 cm (1 in) wide from a newspaper. Fold the strip in half. Hold the strip at its fold with the free ends below.

Use the thumb and index fingers of your other hand to stroke the two halves of the strip.

Results and Conclusions

Why do the two halves fly apart after stroking even though you bring them together when you stroke them?

CHAPTER 2

Moving Charges

In Chapter 1 you saw that electric charges can be separated. For example, a rubber balloon acquires charge when rubbed with a woolen cloth. The cloth acquires the opposite charge. Because the charges on these objects are at rest, they are referred to as static charge. In this chapter, you will investigate charges that move.

Figures 4a and 4b demonstrate how we know that charges can move. One electroscope has been charged negatively by touching it with a rubber rod that has been rubbed with fur. A second electroscope is positively charged. It has been touched with a glass rod that was rubbed with silk. If these two electroscopes are connected by an insulated wire, both electroscopes

◄Electricity is carried from generation plants to buildings throughout the country on high-voltage transmission lines.

discharge (lose their charge). In order to discharge, the charges must have moved from one electroscope to the other. This experiment does not tell us whether positive charges flow to negative charges, negative charges flow to positive charges, or both types of charge move. But it does show that one or both kinds of charge can move from one place to another.

Of course, it is not practical to keep charging electroscopes in order to obtain moving charges. Normally, we use batteries or generators to move charge. A battery is a device that can produce an electric current, a flow of electric charge. Figure 4c shows how a battery can be used to force charge onto an electroscope. In a later chapter, you will investigate how batteries and generators work.

In this chapter, you will move charges and create electric circuits by using batteries. An electric circuit is a complete path along which charges may flow from one pole of a battery to the other. The electric circuits you will make consist of a battery, wires along which charges move, and various devices such as lightbulbs and motors that will react to current from the battery.

Figure 4.

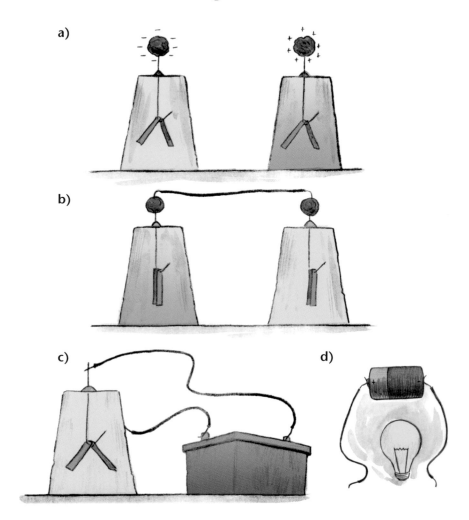

a)

b)

c)   d)

a) One electroscope is negatively charged. A second electroscope is
   positively charged.
b) When the two electroscopes are connected by an insulated wire with
   bare ends, the electroscopes discharge.
c) A battery can be used to charge an electroscope.
d) Can you light a flashlight bulb by touching it with two wires connected
   to a D cell?

EXPERIMENT 2.1

A Simple Electric Circuit

Question:

How does an electric circuit cause a lightbulb to light?

Hypothesis:

The circuit allows electric energy to flow to and from the bulb.

Materials:

- **an adult**
- 2 insulated wires about 15 cm (6 in) long
- wire stripper or knife
- a partner
- D cell (flashlight battery)
- flashlight bulb

Procedure:

1. Obtain two insulated wires, each about 15 cm (6 in) long. **Ask an adult** to strip away about 3 cm (1 in) of insulation from each end of the wires.

2. Have a partner hold one end of each of the two wires firmly against the metal ends of the D cell (flashlight battery), as shown in Figure 4d. **Your partner's fingers should not touch the bare wire or the battery poles.** The poles of the cell are probably marked + (positive) and – (negative). If not, the end with the small cylindrical projection is the positive pole.

3. While your partner holds the ends of the two wires against the poles of the D cell, bring the other ends of the wires to the bulb. **Do not touch the bare wires or the metal on the bulb.**

Results and Conclusions

At what two places do you have to touch the bulb to make it light?

You know how to connect the bulb to the battery using two wires to make a circuit. How can you light the bulb using just one wire to form the circuit?

 Science Project Ideas

- Take a flashlight apart. Can you figure out how it works?

- Build a flashlight of your own design.

EXPERIMENT 2.2

Building Circuits

Question:

How is the brightness of a lightbulb affected by the amount of electrical energy it conducts?

Hypothesis:

The more electricity a lightbulb conducts, the brighter its light will be.

Materials:

- **an adult**
- paper clips
- wire stripper
- thumbtacks
- D cell
- battery holders and bulb holders
- insulated wires (with alligator clips if available)
- soft wood block
- strong, wide rubber bands
- clothespins

Holding wires against battery poles and bulbs is a clumsy and tiring way to build electric circuits. If you have battery holders, bulb holders, and wires with alligator clips like those shown in Figure 5a, you can assemble circuits quickly. If you do not have this equipment, you can make your own from wood, rubber bands, paper clips, thumbtacks, and clothespins (see Figure 5b).

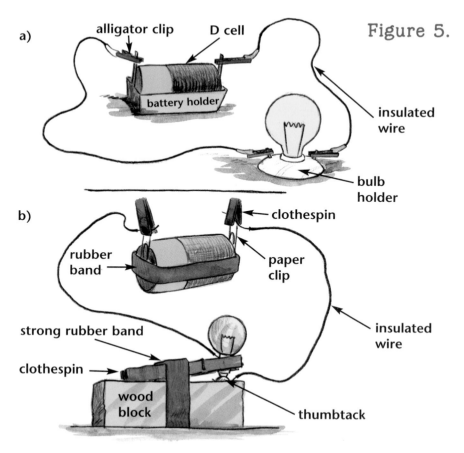

a) An electric circuit is easy to build if you have battery and bulb holders and wires with alligator clips.

b) You can make your own battery and bulb holders using paper clips, rubber bands, thumbtacks, wood blocks, and clothespins.

Procedure:

1. If you build your own equipment, put the bare end of a wire under the thumbtack in your soft-wood bulb holder. Press the thumbtack firmly against the wood. This will hold the wire in place and make it unnecessary to move it.

2. The clothespin holding the bulb can then be fixed to the wood block with a strong rubber band. The metal tab at the bottom of the bulb should rest firmly against the thumbtack.

3. A second wire can be inserted between the clothespin and the metal that surrounds the bulb just below the glass part of the bulb.

4. A battery holder can be made from a strong, wide rubber band that holds paper clips against the poles of a D cell. Clothespins can be used to hold the bare ends of wires against the paper clips.

   Most diagrams of electrical circuits do not show all the details of the equipment that you see in Figure 5. Instead a simple code is used. A bulb, for example, is represented by a circle with a zigzag line across it. The circle represents the glass part of the bulb; the zigzag line represents the thin filament that glows when charge flows through it. The various symbols used to represent parts of a circuit are shown in Figure 6.

5. Use the symbols in Figure 6 to build the circuits shown in Figure 7. In Figure 7d, two D cells can be connected head to tail by using a somewhat longer rubber band or by using a wire to connect the positive (+) pole of one D cell to the negative (−) pole, or terminal, of a second.

Figure 6.

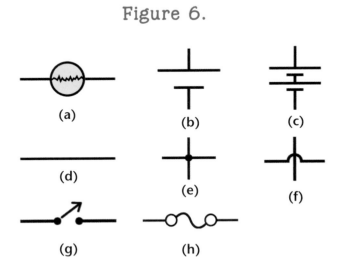

In drawing electric circuits, the parts may be represented by these symbols.
a) a bulb; b) an electric cell (a battery); c) two cells connected head (+) to tail (−); d) a wire; e) wires that are joined; f) wires that cross but are not joined; g) a switch; h) a fuse.

6. In Figure 7b, the D cell has been turned around from its position in 7a. Does turning the cell around affect the brightness of the bulb?

7. In Figure 7c, a second bulb has been added to the circuit shown in 7a. Does adding a second bulb affect the brightness of the bulbs?

8. In Figure 7d, a second D cell has been added. Does the addition of a second electric cell affect the brightness of the bulb?

Results and Conclusions

How does the brightness of the two bulbs in Figure 7e compare with the brightness of the bulb in Figure 7a? Do you think the bulb in Figure 7f will light? Why or why not? Try it.

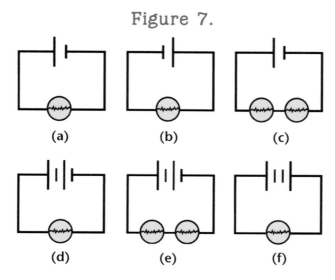

Figure 7.

(a)   (b)   (c)

(d)   (e)   (f)

Use the symbols shown in Figure 6 to build each of the six circuits shown here.

 Science Project Idea

• Design and build some battery and bulb holders of your own.

EXPERIMENT 2.3

Series and Parallel Circuits

Question:

Does the electrical energy in all circuits always stop flowing when it is cut in one or more places?

Hypothesis:

No, in parallel circuits the energy flows even when cut in all but one place.

Materials:

- 3 flashlight bulbs
- 3 bulb holders
- 2 D cells
- battery holder
- insulated wires

Procedure:

1. Arrange three flashlight bulbs as shown in Figure 8a. When bulbs are arranged in this way, they are said to be wired in series, one after the other.

2. After you have built the circuit, connect it to two D cells in series, as shown. What happens if you unscrew one of the bulbs? Does it matter which one you unscrew? How can you explain what you have observed?

3. Now build the circuit shown in Figure 8b. When bulbs are arranged side by side like those in Figure 8b, they are said to be wired in parallel. Why do you think they are said to be wired in parallel?

4. After you have built this parallel circuit, unscrew one of the bulbs. What happens? Does it matter which bulb you unscrew? How can you explain what you have observed?

5. Build the circuits shown in Figure 8c.

Figure 8.

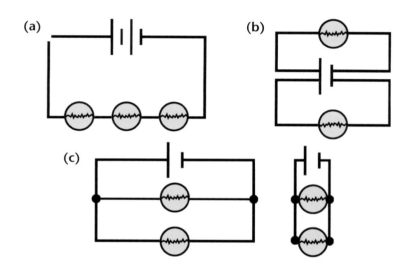

a) A circuit with three lightbulbs wired in series.
b) A circuit with two lightbulbs wired in parallel.
c) Are the bulbs in these circuits wired in series or in parallel?

Results and Conclusions

Are the bulbs in Figure 8c in series or in parallel? How can you find out?

 Science Project Idea

• How do you know that the circuit elements in your home or school are wired in parallel? What would happen if they were wired in series?

EXPERIMENT 2.4

Switches

Question:
How does an electrical switch work?

Hypothesis:
A switch can either allow or interrupt the flow of electricity in a circuit.

Materials:
- 3 small blocks of soft wood
- thumbtacks
- paper clips
- ruler
- insulated wires
- household wall switch (obtain from hardware store)

In your house, you use a switch to turn a light on or off. You can make a simple switch to insert in a circuit using a small block of wood, two thumbtacks, and a paper clip (see Figure 9a).

Figure 9.

(a)

(b)

(c)

a) Make a switch using thumbtacks, a paper clip, and a wood block.
b) Insert the switch into a circuit. Use it to turn the lightbulb
   on and off.
c) Build a pair of switches that will allow you to turn the bulb on
   and off at two locations.

Procedure:

1. Bend a paper clip into an S shape. Push two thumbtacks partway into
   the wood. They should be about 5 cm (2 in) apart.

2. Wrap the bare ends of two separate wires around the thumbtacks.
   Push one of the thumbtacks down firmly to hold the wire in place.
   Slide one end of the paper clip under the second thumbtack before you
   push it firmly into the wood.

3. You can close the switch by pushing the bent end of the paper clip down onto the head of the first thumbtack. Open the switch by releasing the paper clip.

4. Now build the circuit shown in Figure 9b. Use the switch to turn the light on and off. How is this switch different from the ones you find in your home?

5. If you have a wall switch like those used in your home, insert it into the circuit in place of your paper-clip switch. How should you connect the wires to the switch?

6. In your home, you can probably find switches that turn a light on from two different locations. For example, a light at the top of a stairway can usually be turned on or off at both the top and bottom of the stairs. To see how such switches work, build a pair of switches like those shown in Figure 9c. In these switches, the paper clips should be flat so they can touch two thumbtacks at the same time.

Results and Conclusions

How can you use either switch to turn the light on and off?

 Science Project Ideas

- Can you build switches that will allow you to turn a lightbulb on and off from three different locations?

- Ask an electrician to show you how he wires switches that can turn a light on or off from two different places in a building.

EXPERIMENT 2.5

Flow of Charge Around a Circuit

Question:

Is an electrical charge used up as it flows around a circuit?

Hypothesis:

No, all the charge flows all the way around the circuit and is not used up.

Materials:

- 3 identical bulbs (GE #41 or GE #48 bulbs work well)
- 2 D cells
- insulated wires
- battery holder
- 3 bulb holders

People often think that charge gets used up as it flows around a circuit. However, it is quite easy to show that charge is not used up. All the charge flows all the way around the circuit. To see that this is true, build the circuit shown in Figure 10. It has three identical bulbs wired one after the other and connected to two D cells.

Procedure:

1. Connect the battery of two D cells to the bulbs.

2. Compare the brightness of the three bulbs.

Figure 10.

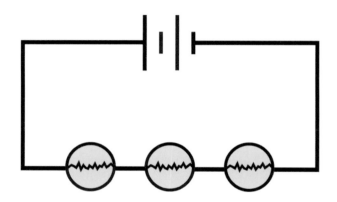

How does the brightness of three identical bulbs wired in series compare?

Results and Conclusions

If charge were used up as it flows around the circuit, how would the brightness of the three bulbs compare? Using a battery of two D cells, how many bulbs can be connected one after the other before the bulbs do not light? If the bulbs do not light, does that mean that no charge is flowing? Or could it be that there is simply not enough charge to make the bulbs glow?

EXPERIMENT 2.6

Sending Messages Electrically

Question:

What is the principle behind Morse code?

Hypothesis:

Longer and shorter electrical impulses can be arranged to symbolize letters of the alphabet.

Materials:

- D cells
- battery holder
- flashlight bulbs
- bulb holders
- long insulated wires
- switches from Experiment 2.4
- a friend

In 1844, Samuel F. B. Morse sent the first long-distance telegraph message over a wire that led from Washington, D.C., to Baltimore, Maryland. He used a code he had invented of dots and dashes. That code, still known as Morse code, is shown in Figure 11. The code also includes periods, commas, and question marks, but you may find it more fun to invent your own code for these punctuation marks.

Figure 11.

A) • —
B) — • • •
C) — • — •
D) — • •
E) •
F) • • — •
G) — — •
H) • • • •
I) • •
J) • — — —
K) — • —
L) • — • •
M) — —

N) — •
O) — — —
P) • — — •
Q) — — • —
R) • — •
S) • • •
T) —
U) • • —
V) • • • —
W) • — —
X) — • • —
Y) — • — —
Z) — — • •

1) • — — — —
2) • • — — —
3) • • • — —
4) • • • • —
5) • • • • •
6) — • • • •
7) — — • • •
8) — — — • •
9) — — — — •
0) — — — — —
,) — — • • — —
.) • — • — • —
?) • • — — • •

Morse code consists of dots and dashes that can be made with either light or sound signals.

Procedure:

1. You can use the code, together with an electric circuit, to send messages to a friend in another room. Pressing the switch shown in Figure 12 will cause both the bulb in your room and the bulb in the next room to light. Pressing the switch for a short time will produce a dot. Pressing the switch for a longer time will produce a dash.

2. A similar circuit can be used by your friend to send signals to you.

Figure 12.

You can send coded messages using a simple electric circuit.

Results and Conclusions

At first, you will want to keep the code in front of you as you send messages. Later, with practice, you will find that you have learned the code and can send messages more rapidly without looking at the chart.

 Science Project Ideas

- Design and build a *single* circuit that will allow both you and your friend to send and receive messages.

- Prepare demonstrations to show how Sir Charles Wheatstone, Samuel Morse, and Joseph Henry were involved in the invention and use of the telegraph.

EXPERIMENT 2.7

Short Circuit: The Easy Path

Question:

Why is an alternative route followed by an electric charge termed a short circuit?

Hypothesis:

The charge is following an easier path, taking a "shortcut," rather than following the intended, longer, circuit.

Materials:

- 2 D cells
- battery holder
- flashlight bulb
- bulb holder
- insulated wires
- piece of bare (uninsulated) wire

Procedure:

1. Build a simple circuit like the one shown in Figure 13a.

2. What happens to the flashlight bulb when you touch the ends of a bare (uninsulated) wire to the poles of the D cell as shown in Figure 13b?

3. What happens to the bulb if you use the same bare wire to touch both leads to the bulb as shown in Figure 13c?

Figure 13.

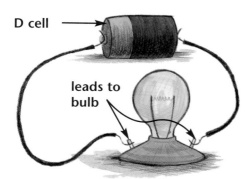

D cell

leads to bulb

bulb

a) Top view of a simple circuit.

bare wire

D cell

b) What happens to the bulb when you touch the poles of the D cell with the ends of a bare wire?

D cell

bare wire

c) What happens to the bulb when you place a bare wire across its leads?

Results and Conclusions

The bulb lights when electric charges flow from the D cell, through the bulb, and back to the D cell. However, if you provide an alternate path, one that allows charges to flow more easily, the charges will take the easier path. When faced with riding your bike up a steep hill or along a level path, you would probably choose the level path even though it may be a longer ride. It is the easier path for you. Similarly, charges move more easily along a wire, even a long wire, than through a bulb's short filament.

Procedure:

1. If you have a D cell you can spare, connect the ends of a bare (uninsulated) wire to it. After several minutes, feel the D cell. What do you notice?

2. After an hour, remove the wire and connect the cell to a bulb. How does the brightness of the bulb compare to the brightness of an identical bulb connected to a new D cell?

Results and Conclusions

As you will find, a D cell wears out quickly when its poles are connected to a plain wire. Such a connection creates what is called a short circuit. Because most of the charge flows through the short circuit, there is little charge left to flow through whatever else may be connected to the cell. When building circuits, be careful not to create short circuits. Your cells will wear out very quickly if you do.

Examine the circuits in Figure 14. In which circuits will the bulb (or bulbs) light? In which are there short circuits? If you are not sure, build the circuit and find out.

Figure 14.

Which bulbs will light? Where do you find short circuits? Where do you find bulbs that will not light even though there are no short circuits?

EXPERIMENT 2.8

Resistors: The Hard Path

Question:
What do resistors do?

Hypothesis:
Resistors have many functions in electrical equipment—the most common being to reduce the amount of charge flowing through a circuit.

Materials:
- insulated wires
- flashlight bulb
- bulb socket
- D cell
- battery holder
- thumbtacks
- sheet of cardboard
- 60-cm (24-in) length of #30 (thin) Nichrome wire
- 60-cm (24-in) length of #26 (thick) Nichrome wire

Procedure:

1. Build the circuit shown in Figure 15a. One insulated wire (wire X) leads from a D cell to a flashlight bulb. The end of a second wire from the D cell (wire Z) is left unconnected. A wire leading from the bulb (wire Y) is also unconnected.

Figure 15.

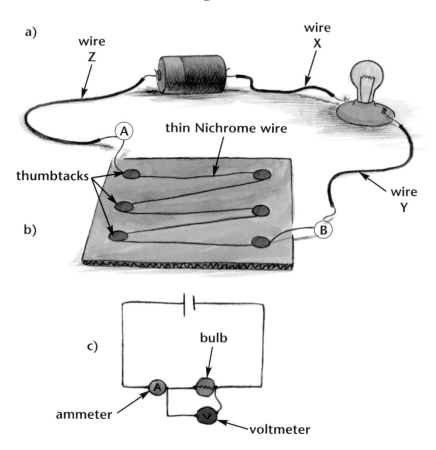

a) Build the circuit shown here.

b) Run a 60-cm- (24-in-) length of Nichrome wire back and forth along a sheet of cardboard. What effect does the Nichrome wire have on the brightness of the bulb? How does the length of the Nichrome wire affect the bulb's brightness?

c) Using a voltmeter and an ammeter, you can find the resistance of a lightbulb.

2. Next, connect a 60-cm (24-in) length of thin Nichrome wire between points A and B. Nichrome is a combination of chromium, nickel, and iron commonly used in heating elements.

3. You can run the Nichrome wire back and forth several times around thumbtacks stuck in a sheet of cardboard as shown in Figure 15b.

4. Connect the end of wire Y to one end of the Nichrome wire. Connect the end of wire Z to the other end of the Nichrome wire. By sliding the end of wire Y along the Nichrome wire, you can vary the length of the Nichrome wire between A and B.

Results and Conclusions

How does the length of Nichrome wire between A and B affect the brightness of the bulb?

What does the brightness of the bulb tell you about the amount of charge flowing through the bulb? How does increasing the length of Nichrome wire in the circuit affect the amount of charge flowing around the circuit?

How do you think the results would change if you used a thicker piece of Nichrome wire? Try it! What do you find?

Given equal lengths of Nichrome wire, which offers more resistance to charge flow, the thick or the thin wire?

As you have seen, Nichrome wire, when placed in a circuit, reduces the amount of charge that flows through the circuit. The wire resists the flow of charge because of the elements of which it is made.

The filaments in an incandescent bulb are made of tungsten. Tungsten, too, offers resistance to charge flow. A very high temperature is needed to melt tungsten. Consequently, lightbulb filaments can be heated until they glow with a white light without melting.

Every element in an electric circuit, such as a bulb, a motor, even a D cell, offers some resistance to charge flow. Sometimes elements called resistors are purposely placed in a circuit to reduce the amount of charge flowing through the circuit.

Science Project Ideas

- The resistance of a resistor, lightbulb, or any element in a circuit is defined as the voltage across the element divided by the current through it. Voltage, which is measured in volts, is found by using a voltmeter. Current, which is measured in units called amperes, is found by using an ammeter. An ammeter measures the number of charges per second flowing through a circuit. To measure the resistance of a lightbulb in a circuit, you can build the circuit shown in Figure 15c. As you can see, the ammeter is placed in series with the bulb. The voltmeter is placed in parallel with the bulb.

  Resistance is measured in ohms; one ohm equals one volt per ampere.

$$1 \text{ ohm} = 1 \text{ volt/ampere}$$

  What is the resistance of the lightbulb according to your measurements?

- Does the resistance of a lightbulb's filament change with temperature? Design and conduct an experiment to find out.

EXPERIMENT 2.9

A Burglar Alarm Circuit

Question:

Are electrical devices always extremely complex?

Hypothesis:

No, the fundamental principle of the circuit is simple, but it can be used for many important purposes.

Materials:

- piece of cardboard about 15 cm (6 in) by 8 cm (3 in)
- strips of aluminum foil about 3 cm (1 in) wide
- tape
- long insulated wires with bare ends
- 2-D-cell battery
- buzzer (buy at an electronics store)
- carpet or mat

You can build a simple alarm that can be used to detect anyone who enters your house or room. You will need a piece of cardboard about 15 cm (6 in) by 8 cm (3 in).

Procedure:

1. Make a fold line in the cardboard at its center as shown in Figure 16a.

2. Wrap strips of aluminum foil about 3 cm (1 in) wide around the cardboard as shown. Then place the bare ends of two long insulated wires on the aluminum strips. Use tape to fasten the wire to the aluminum strips, and the aluminum to the cardboard.

3. Finish folding the cardboard, being sure the aluminum strips do not touch.

Figure 16a.

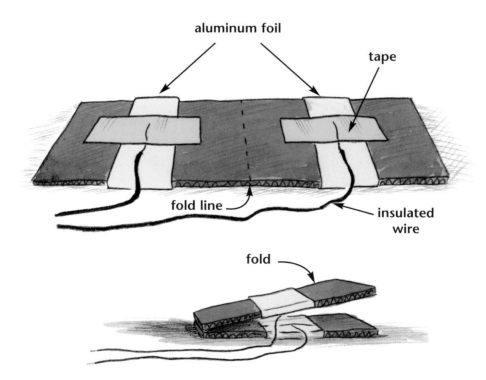

4. Place the folded cardboard under a carpet or mat near a door. Be sure the weight of the carpet does not squeeze the aluminum strips together.

5. Next, connect the wires you taped to the aluminum foil to a 2-D-cell battery and a buzzer, forming the circuit shown in Figure 16b.

Results and Conclusions

When someone steps on the carpet, it will force the aluminum strips together. This will close the circuit and activate the buzzer, letting you know that a person has entered your home or your room.

Figure 16b.

You can build an alarm that will alert you when people enter your home or room.

EXPERIMENT 2.10

A Fuse for Safety

Question:

How does a fuse work?

Hypothesis:

The fuse—the basic safety element used in an electric circuit—cuts off electricity in a circuit that is becoming too hot.

Materials:

- clay
- 3 thick pieces of bare copper wire
- steel wool
- 2-D-cell battery
- insulated wires
- flashlight bulb and bulb holder

Homes with old electrical wiring may have fuses. In modern homes, fuses have been replaced with circuit breakers. Fuses are widely used in automobile electrical systems and in household appliances. The purpose of a fuse is to prevent a circuit from becoming so hot that it could start a fire.

You can build a circuit with a fuse to see how it works.

Procedure:

1. Use a piece of clay to support two thick pieces of copper wire upright and about half a centimeter apart.

2. Remove a single strand of wire from a pad of steel wool. Wrap the ends of the steel wire firmly around the ends of the two upright copper wires, as shown in Figure 17a.

a) A fuse is connected to a 2-D-cell battery. What will happen?
b) What happens to the fuse when there is a bulb in the circuit?
   A bulb and a short in the circuit?

3. Build the circuit shown. The thin steel wire will be the fuse in this circuit.

4. When you connect the fuse to the 2-D-cell battery, you will see what happens to a fuse when a large current flows through it. In a typical circuit, the fuse should not blow.

5. Rebuild the circuit with a flashlight bulb between the battery and the fuse. When you connect this circuit, the fuse should not blow. The bulb's resistance reduces the flow of current. With less charge flowing through the fuse, the fuse does not get hot enough to melt. (If it does melt, use a single D cell rather than two.)

6. What happens when there is a short circuit? To find out, touch both ends of a short length of bare copper wire to the connections leading to and from the bulb, as shown in Figure 17b. Is the resistance of the copper wire large or small? What happens to the fuse?

Predict what will happen if you rebuild the circuit and connect the bare copper wire to the poles of the battery. Try it! Was your prediction right?

Results and Conclusions

Fuses have to be replaced when they blow. The circuit breakers used in wiring homes today simply have to be reset. Circuit breakers are based on a relationship between electricity and magnetism, which you will explore in the next chapter.

EXPERIMENT 3.1

Two Magnets

Question:

What happens when the poles of two magnets are brought together?

Hypothesis:

The opposite poles will attract each other while the like poles will repel.

Materials:

- thread
- tape
- 2 bar magnets or square or circular ceramic magnets
- pen and small piece of masking tape (if needed to mark magnets)
- toothpick
- magnetic compass
- drinking straw or stick
- clay
- several square or circular ceramic magnets with holes in their centers

Procedure:

1. Use thread and tape to suspend a bar magnet or a square or circular ceramic magnet. If you use a small square or circular magnet, tape a toothpick to the magnet as shown in Figure 18. Notice that once the magnet stops turning, it always points in a northerly direction. If it does not point in a northerly direction, there are other magnetic materials nearby. Move the experiment to a point far from any metallic material.

Figure 18.

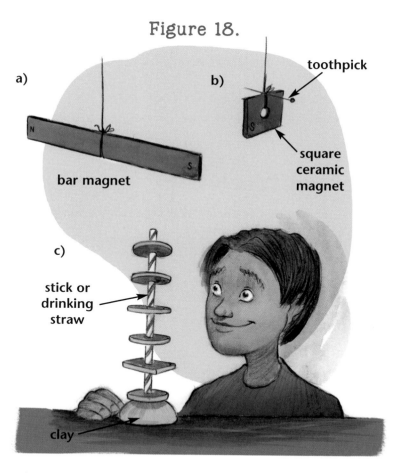

Suspend a bar magnet (a) or a square or round ceramic magnet (b) by a thread. Notice that the magnet always points in the same direction. (c) Can you make a set of floating magnets like these?

2. Once the suspended magnet is at rest, mark the end or side that is northernmost with an N if it is not already marked. Mark the other end or side with an S.

3. Repeat the process with a second magnet. Again, if not already marked, mark the northernmost side or end with an N and the southernmost end or side with an S. The ends or sides of the magnets that you have marked N or S are called poles. The pole marked N is the north-seeking pole of the magnet. The pole marked S is the south-seeking pole.

4. What happens when you bring the north-seeking pole of one magnet near the north-seeking pole of a second magnet?

5. What happens when you bring the north-seeking pole of one magnet near the south-seeking pole of a second magnet?

Results and Conclusions

Predict what will happen when you bring the south-seeking pole of one magnet near the south-seeking pole of a second magnet. Try it! Was your prediction correct?

What can you conclude about the force between like poles of two magnets? What can you conclude about the force between opposite (N and S) poles of two magnets?

What do you think will happen if you slowly bring the north-seeking pole of a magnet near the north-seeking pole of a compass needle? Try it! Were you right?

What do you think will happen if you slowly bring the south-seeking pole of a magnet near the north-seeking pole of a compass needle?

Obtain several square or circular ceramic magnets with holes in their centers. Figure out a way to place these magnets on a drinking straw or stick so that they float like the ones shown in Figure 18c.

 Science Project Ideas

- You can turn a nail into a magnet. Hold the nail against a piece of wood with one hand. Use the other hand to stroke the entire length of the nail with a bar magnet. Apply all strokes in the same direction and with the same pole of the magnet. After about 30 strokes, test the nail to see if it behaves like a magnet. If it does, how does its polarity compare with the pole you used to stroke the nail?

- Having made a magnet, investigate ways to remove its magnetic properties.

- To make a simple compass, like ones used by ancient sailors, turn a sewing needle into a magnet by stroking it with a bar magnet. Remove the bottom from a Styrofoam cup and put it in a bowl of water. Place the needle on the Styrofoam disk. Does the needle behave like a magnetic compass?

- Use your ingenuity to make a variety of magnetic compasses from ordinary materials you can find in your home or school.

Earth as a Magnet

The fact that a compass needle points in a northerly direction suggests that Earth behaves like a giant magnet, as shown in Figure 19. Suppose you were to take a compass to the Boothia Peninsula, north of Hudson Bay, in northern Canada, about 1,200 miles from Earth's geographic North Pole. There, at about 76 degrees latitude, 100 degrees west longitude, you would find the compass needle points straight down, indicating it is over one of Earth's magnetic poles. But think! If the north-seeking pole of your compass points downward at this pole, is Earth's magnetic pole under Boothia Peninsula a north-seeking or a south-seeking pole?

Similarly, suppose you took a compass to a point in Antarctica near Dumont d'Urville, about 1,200 miles from Earth's geographic South Pole. There, at about 67 degrees latitude, 140 degrees east longitude, you would find the compass needle's north-seeking pole pointing straight up. Is Earth's magnetic pole in Antarctica a north-seeking or a south-seeking pole?

Since Earth's magnetic poles are not located at its north and south geographic poles, compass needles seldom point toward true north. Within half a degree, the North Star is directly above our North Pole. At night, a compass needle is not likely to point in the direction of the North Star. For example, a compass near Boston, Massachusetts, will point about 15 degrees west of true geographic north. A compass near San Diego, California, will point about 15 degrees east of true geographic north. But there are points where a compass needle does point toward true north. Such a region lies along the Georgia-South Carolina border.

The difference between true geographic north and magnetic north is called the magnetic declination. However, Earth's magnetism is constantly

Figure 19.

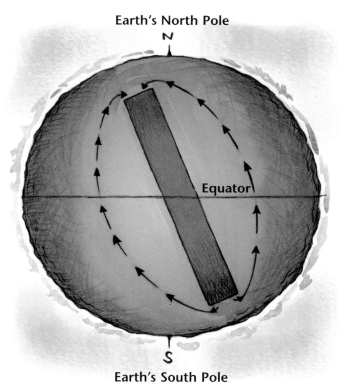

Earth's North Pole
N

Equator

S
Earth's South Pole

Earth behaves as if it contained a giant magnet. The small arrows show the general direction of compass needles at various points on Earth's surface. At a point in the northern hemisphere, above one of Earth's magnetic poles, a compass needle will point straight down toward the ground.

changing. Therefore, charts showing the angles of magnetic declination on Earth's surface have to be revised frequently.

Around every magnet, including whatever acts like a magnet inside Earth, there is a magnetic field. We cannot see the field, but it can be mapped and its force revealed by compass needles. You will map a magnetic field in the next experiment.

EXPERIMENT 3.2

A Magnetic Field

Question:

How can you demonstrate the presence of a magnetic field?

Hypothesis:

By spreading iron filings near bar magnets, you will see the patterns of magnetic field attraction or repulsion.

Materials:

- 2 bar magnets
- sheets of white paper
- pencil
- magnetic compass
- iron filings
- scissors (optional)
- ruler
- steel wool (optional)
- old salt or pepper shaker (optional)
- tape
- thin sheet of cardboard

In the early 1800s, Michael Faraday, an English scientist, experimented with electricity and magnetism. He found it useful to think of magnets as if they were surrounded by lines of force. If a compass needle is placed near a magnet, it will point in a particular direction. To Faraday, the compass needle near a magnet revealed the direction of the line of force at the location of the compass. The magnetic field around the magnet consisted of all the lines of force.

You can map the lines of force around a bar magnet.

Procedure:

1. Place the magnet on a sheet of white paper. Use a pencil to mark the direction a compass needle points as the compass is moved around the magnet (see Figure 20a). The direction of a magnetic field at any point is defined as the direction given by the north-seeking end of a compass needle. Begin with the compass near the south pole of the magnet. Simply move the compass to an adjacent position in the direction the compass needle was pointing. Repeat this process until you reach the magnet's north pole.

   You could repeat this a number of times to obtain the entire field around the magnet. However, there is an easier way to reveal the field around a magnet. Iron filings, small pieces of iron, behave like tiny compass needles. You can probably obtain iron filings from a science teacher or a hobby shop. If not, you can make your own.

2. Over a sheet of paper, use scissors to cut part of a roll of steel wool into tiny pieces.

3. Use the paper to pour the particles into an old salt or pepper shaker.

4. Once you have some iron filings, tape a sheet of white paper to a thin sheet of cardboard. Place the cardboard on top of a bar magnet. Then sprinkle some iron filings over the paper.

5. Tap the cardboard gently. The filings will align themselves like tiny compass needles, revealing the field lines about the bar magnet. Does the field resemble the one shown in Figure 20b?

6. To see the pattern near repelling magnetic poles, tape two bar magnets in place with their north-seeking poles about 5 cm (2 in) apart (see Figure 20c). Use paper, cardboard, and iron filings to examine the magnetic field pattern near repelling poles.

7. Repeat the experiment to find the magnetic field pattern between attracting magnetic poles.

Figure 20.

a) A small compass can be used to map lines of force
    (field lines) around a bar magnet.
b) A magnetic field is revealed by iron filings.
c) What does the field near repelling poles look like?

Results and Conclusions

Because a compass needle on Earth points in a particular direction, we know there is a magnetic field above Earth. The pattern of this field is similar to the field you found around a bar magnet. Suppose you were to follow one of Earth's magnetic field lines as indicated by a compass needle. Where would your journey take you?

 Science Project Ideas

- Design and carry out an experiment to find out whether or not the tiny particles in an iron-enriched cereal will respond to a magnet.

- Prepare a mixture of iron filings, salt, and sawdust. Design an experiment to separate the three components of the mixture.

- Which part of a bar magnet is stronger, the poles or the middle? Design and conduct an experiment to find out.

- Place two bar magnets in a line about 10 cm (4 in) apart with their north poles facing each other. Place a small compass between the poles. Find a point at which the compass needle is not turned toward either pole. (The needle is at a right angle to an imaginary line connecting the two poles.) Why does such a point between repelling poles exist? Is there a similar point for poles that attract?

- How can you use waxed paper and iron filings to prepare permanent magnetic field patterns?

EXPERIMENT 3.3

Magnets, Magnetic Matter, and Nonmagnetic Matter

Question:

Is every material a magnet if it is attracted by a magnet?

Hypothesis:

No, some materials are only "magnetic" when they are in reach of a magnet's magnetic field.

Materials:

- tape
- thread
- 2 magnets
- magnetic compass
- piece of wood
- small test tube
- iron filings
- paper clip
- a cork
- a variety of objects such as steel, copper, or aluminum nails, brass screws or tacks, cardboard, tin, aluminum cans, wooden pencils, etc.

You have seen that a magnet has two poles (N and S). You have also demonstrated that like poles (N-N or S-S) repel and unlike poles (N-S) attract. You can use what you know to classify various materials into three groups: magnets, magnetic matter, and nonmagnetic matter. A magnet will both attract and repel another magnet. Magnetic matter can be magnetized. Such matter is attracted by a magnet but is not a magnet itself. Once the attracting magnet is removed, the matter will not behave like a magnet. Finally, nonmagnetic matter is not affected by a magnet. It is neither attracted nor repelled by a magnet.

Procedure:

1. Use tape and thread to suspend a magnet.

2. Bring a variety of objects near the magnet. You might try such things as another magnet; nails made of steel, copper, or aluminum; plastic; glass; brass screws or tacks; cardboard; paper; tin cans (actually steel coated with tin); aluminum cans; plastic wrap; aluminum foil; wax paper; brass; rubber bands or erasers; wooden pencils; plastic rulers; paper clips; thumbtacks; and whatever else you can find.

Results and Conclusions

Which of the materials attracted the magnet? Did any repel the magnet? If something attracted the magnet, did you turn it around to see if it would repel the magnet? Classify the materials you tested into things that are magnets, magnetic matter, and nonmagnetic matter.

Sometimes magnetic matter can be made into a magnet.

Procedure:

1. Hold a paper clip near a magnetic compass. The paper clip should have no effect on the compass needle. If it does, choose another paper clip.

2. Next, hold the paper clip against a piece of wood. Then stroke the entire length of the paper clip with a bar magnet. Apply all strokes in the same direction and with the same pole of the magnet.

3. After about 30 strokes, bring the paper clip near a magnetic compass. Does one end of the paper clip act like a south-seeking pole, while the other end acts like a north-seeking pole?

4. Fill a small test tube with iron filings. Put a cork in the tube so that the filings cannot fall out.

5. Again, stroke the entire length of the test tube with a bar magnet as you did the paper clip. Carefully pick up the test tube in a horizontal position. Bring the test tube close to a magnetic compass.

Results and Conclusions

Has the test tube of filings become a magnet? If it has, which end is the north pole? The south pole?

Carefully put the test tube aside for use in the next experiment.

EXPERIMENT 3.4

Unmaking a Magnet

Question:

Can you "demagnetize" a magnet?

Hypothesis:

Yes, you can "unmake" a magnet by jarring its atoms from their magnetized alignments.

Materials:

- **an adult**
- small test tube with iron filings from Experiment 3.3
- magnetic compass
- paper clips
- a strong magnet
- thread
- hard floor
- hammer
- pliers
- candle
- matches
- piece of wood

As you have seen, a magnet can be made by stroking a piece of iron or steel with a strong magnet. The reason this works is that the atoms of certain elements such as iron each behave like tiny magnets. In an unmagnetized piece of iron, the atoms are arranged in a random fashion. As a result, the tiny magnets cancel one another's magnetism, as shown in Figure 21a. When the iron is properly stroked with a magnet, the atoms are forced to line up with more of their poles pointing in one direction than any other, as shown in Figure 21b.

Most magnets are made of steel or an alloy of nickel, cobalt, aluminum, and iron. Ceramic magnets are made by embedding oxides of iron, nickel, and beryllium in clay. These magnets are called permanent magnets because they retain their magnetism.

Are there ways to demagnetize magnets? You might guess that jarring the atoms from their alignment would destroy their magnetism. Perhaps dropping the magnets would demagnetize them or at least reduce their strength.

Figure 21.

a)

b)

a) The magnetic atoms in an unmagnetized piece of iron are arranged in a random manner. As a result their magnetic effects cancel one another.
b) When magnetized, the poles of the atoms are aligned, creating a strong magnetic field.

Procedure:

1. Hold the small test tube of iron filings from Experiment 3.3 and thoroughly shake it several times.

2. Bring the test tube close to a magnetic compass. Has the tube of filings lost all or most of its magnetism?

3. To further test this idea, magnetize two paper clips by stroking each of them with a strong magnet as you did in Experiment 3.3.

4. Suspend one of the paper-clip magnets from a thread. Bring one pole of the second paper-clip magnet near a pole of the suspended magnet. Do the two poles attract or repel? Use the two paper-clip magnets to show that like poles repel and unlike poles attract.

5. Next, drop both magnetized paper clips on a hard floor several times. Again suspend one paper clip from a thread and bring the second paper clip near the suspended one. Has dropping the paper-clip magnets eliminated or reduced their magnetism?

6. Will hammering magnetized paper clips also demagnetize them? Carry out an experiment to find out.

   When solid substances are heated, their atoms or molecules vibrate more rapidly. Perhaps heating could also cause the atoms in a magnetic material to be jarred out of alignment. This would eliminate or reduce their magnetism.

7. Again magnetize two paper clips by stroking them with a strong magnet. Check, as before, to be sure the paper clips have been magnetized.

8. **Ask an adult** to heat each paper clip by using pliers to hold each paper clip in a candle flame for a few seconds.

9. After the paper clips have cooled, suspend one paper clip from a thread and bring the second paper clip near the suspended one.

Results and Conclusions

Has heating the paper-clip magnets eliminated or reduced their magnetism?

EXPERIMENT 3.5

Can a Magnetic Field Act Through Materials?

Question:

Can magnetic fields pass through matter?

Hypothesis:

Yes, magnetic fields work through many materials, but not all.

Materials:

- bar magnet
- books
- table
- thread
- paper clip
- tape
- scissors

- various materials such as cardboard, paper, plastic, aluminum foil, a tin can lid, glass, a saucer, water-filled saucer, a cookie tin, and coins

You know that a magnetic field can attract or repel magnets or magnetic matter through air. Can such a field act through other kinds of matter?

bar magnet

thread

tape

Figure 22.

Can a magnetic field
act through materials
other than air?

Procedure:

1. Place a bar magnet under the top book in a stack of books resting on a table, as shown in Figure 22. Tie one end of a piece of thread to a paper clip. Tape the other end to the table. The magnet should be strong enough to keep the paper clip suspended, as shown in the drawing.

2. With the magnetic field keeping the paper clip floating below the magnet, place different samples of thin materials between the magnet and the paper clip. You might try pieces of cardboard, paper, plastic, aluminum foil, a tin can lid, glass, a saucer, a water-filled saucer, a cookie tin, and coins.

Results and Conclusions

Through which materials, if any, can the magnetic field pass? Which materials, if any, block the magnetic field? Do you think you can "cut" the field with scissors? Try it! Were you right?

CHAPTER 4

Magnetism From Electricity

As you have seen, electricity and magnetism have much in common. In the case of electricity, like charges (+ and + or − and −) repel each other, and unlike charges (+ and −) attract each other. In the case of magnets, like poles (N and N or S and S) repel each other, and opposite poles (N and S) attract each other. Furthermore, both electric and magnetic forces can be exerted through space; the charges or poles do not have to touch for their effects to be observed.

Because of their similarities, many scientists thought that electricity and magnetism were related. However, until 1819, no one could find a connection between them. That year, Hans Christian Oersted, a Danish physicist, accidentally discovered the connecting link when he brought a magnetic compass near a current-carrying wire. Experiment 4.1 will lead you to the same discovery that Oersted made nearly 200 years ago.

◄A statue to Danish physicist Hans Christian Oersted stands in Copenhagen, Denmark.

EXPERIMENT 4.1

Oersted's Discovery

Question:

How will a magnetic compass be affected by a current-carrying wire?

Hypothesis:

The current's magnetic field will control the compass needle in different ways, depending on the position (placement) of the compass.

Materials:

- magnetic compass
- table or counter
- D cell
- long insulated wire with bare ends

Procedure:

1. Place a magnetic compass on a table or counter. Lay a long insulated wire on top of the compass. The wire should be parallel to the compass needle, as shown in Figure 23.

2. Connect one bared end of the long wire to the pole of a D cell. Briefly touch the other bared end of the wire to the other pole of the D cell. What happens to the compass needle?

Figure 23.

D cell

long insulated wire

What did Oersted discover about the link between electricity and magnetism?

3. Connect the D cell to the wire again and keep current flowing until you can determine the direction the compass needle is pointing. (Do not leave the circuit connected any longer than necessary. The D cell will wear out quickly if it generates a large current.)

   Based on this experiment, what is one connection between electricity and magnetism?

4. Next, put the wire under the compass and repeat the experiment. What happens this time? Is anything different?

5. Leave the wire under the compass and turn the D cell around so that current will flow in the opposite direction.

Results and Conclusions

What do you observe this time when charge flows through the wire?

 Science Project Idea

- In Experiment 3.5, you found that a magnetic field can exert its effects through some kinds of matter such as paper and plastic. Can the magnetic field created by an electric current exert its effect through similar materials? Design an experiment to find out.

EXPERIMENT 4.2

An Electric Current's Magnetic Field

Question:

What are the characteristics of the magnetic field around a wire with a flowing current?

Hypothesis:

The lines of this magnetic field take a circular form around the wire.

Materials:

- long, straight piece of heavy copper wire
- cardboard box
- 4 D cells or 6-volt dry cell battery
- battery holder(s)
- insulated wires
- 1 or more magnetic compasses
- a partner

As you saw in the previous experiment, an electric current produces a magnetic field. But what does the magnetic field around a current look like? What is its direction? Does it resemble the field around a bar magnet?

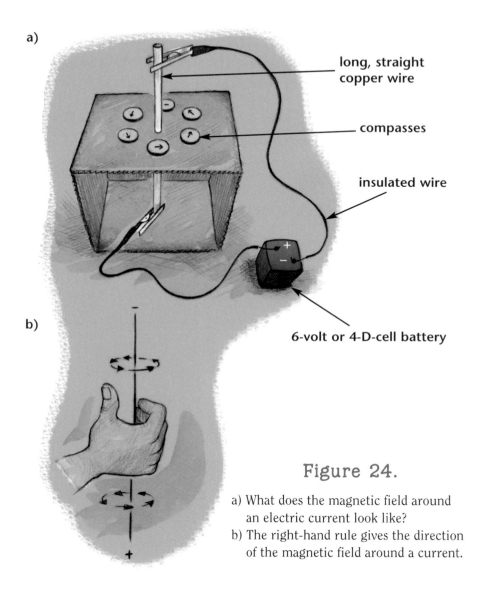

a)

long, straight
copper wire

compasses

insulated wire

6-volt or 4-D-cell battery

b)

Figure 24.

a) What does the magnetic field around
an electric current look like?

b) The right-hand rule gives the direction
of the magnetic field around a current.

Procedure:

1. Push a long, straight piece of heavy copper wire through one side of a
   cardboard box, as shown in Figure 24a. Construct a battery consisting
   of 4 D cells connected end to end, or use a 6-volt dry cell battery.

2. Attach insulated wires to the battery as shown. Briefly connect the ends of the insulated wires to the copper wire. Of course, this is a short circuit, so **it should not be connected for more than a few seconds.**

3. If you have six or more magnetic compasses, place them around the wire as shown. If you only have one compass, have a partner move the compass around the wire while you watch.

Results and Conclusions

As you will see, the magnetic field lines form a circular pattern around the electric current that flows in the wire. The direction of the field lines can be predicted by what is known as the right-hand rule. Point your thumb in the direction that positive charge would flow through the wire. Assume positive charge flows from the battery's positive pole to its negative pole. Your fingers curl in the direction of the magnetic field around the wire. Remember, the direction of a magnetic field is given by the direction the north-seeking pole of a compass needle points. (See Figure 24b.) Do your results agree with this rule?

 Science Project Ideas

- Repeat Experiment 4.2 using iron filings in place of compass needles. What do iron filings reveal more clearly about the pattern? What do they not reveal?

- Based on what you have learned about magnetic fields in Experiments 4.1 and 4.2, how can you explain the existence of Earth's magnetic field?

EXPERIMENT 4.3

An Electric Meter

Question:

What is the basic principle behind the electric meter?

Hypothesis:

The interaction between a current and a magnet allows an electric meter to measure electric current.

Materials:

- **an adult**
- 10 m (33 ft) of
  24-gauge insulated
  wire
- roll of duct tape
- knife or wire stripper
- ruler

- clay or tape
- cardboard
- scissors
- magnetic compass
- insulated wires
- D cell

Since an electric current creates a magnetic field that surrounds the current, it can turn a compass needle, as you have seen. The interaction between an electric current and a magnet can serve as the basis of a meter that can detect electric currents.

Procedure:

1. To make a simple meter, wind about 10 m (33 ft) of 24-gauge insulated wire around a roll of duct tape to make a coil, as shown in Figure 25a. Use some tape to keep the coils in place. Leave about 30 cm (1 ft) of wire at each end of the coil.

2. **Ask an adult** to use a knife or wire stripper to remove about 4 cm (1.5 in) of insulation from each end of the wire. Use clay or tape to support the coil upright as shown.

3. Fold a strip of cardboard to form a platform that will support a compass at the center of the coil. The compass needle should be aligned with (parallel to) the plane of the coils. Use insulated wires to connect the coil to a D cell.

Results and Conclusions

What happens to the compass needle when current flows through the coil? Let the current flow just long enough so that you can see the direction of the magnetic field at the center of the coil. Is this the direction you would expect from the right-hand rule?

Turn the D cell around so that current will flow in the opposite direction. Predict the direction of the magnetic field at the coil's center after making this change. Was your prediction right?

a)
wire coil
wound on roll
of duct tape

cardboard
platform

clay

D cell

b)
wire coil
wound on roll
of duct tape

clay

cardboard
platform

D cell

? ? ?
objects being tested

c)

liquid

Figure 25.

a) You can make a simple meter that
can detect an electric current. The
meter can be used to test the ability
of different materials—(b) solids, (c)
liquids—to conduct charges.

EXPERIMENT 4.4

Using an Electric Meter to Test for Conductivity

Question:

Does an electric meter estimate conductivity?

Hypothesis:

Yes, the meter's compass needle will turn when a material being tested conducts current.

Materials:

- solid objects such as cardboard, nails, plastic, pencils, pencil lead, silverware, wood, paper, coins, candle wax, chalk, glass, rubber bands, paper clips, aluminum foil, and flashlight bulb
- insulated wires
- 4 D cells

- meter from Experiment 4.3
- small plastic medicine cup or vial
- paper clips
- liquids such as water, milk, lemon and other juices, vinegar, carbonated soda, and solutions of salt, sugar, and baking soda

You can use the simple electric meter you built in the previous experiment to find out which materials conduct charge and which do not.

Procedure:

1. Build the circuit shown in Figure 25b. Connect an insulated wire to each end of the D cell. One of these wires should be connected to one end of the coil. The second will be used to touch one side of the object to be tested.

2. Connect a third wire to the other end of the coil; it will be used to touch the other side of the object being tested.

   Solid objects you might test could include cardboard, nails, plastic, pencils, pencil lead, silverware, wood, paper, coins, candle wax, chalk, glass, rubber bands, paper clips, aluminum foil, or a flash-light bulb.

3. To test these solids, touch the ends of the object you are testing with the ends of the two wires, one from the D cell and one from the coil. (**Do not touch for more than a second or two; a large current wears out D cells quickly.**) If the meter's compass needle turns, you know that the material is conducting charge. What will you observe if the item does not conduct charge?

   Which materials are conductors? Which appear to be nonconductors?

Results and Conclusions

From your tests, can you explain why rubber bands were suggested for making battery holders in Experiment 2.2? What would happen if the rubber bands were replaced by metal straps? Why were paper clips used to make contact with the poles of the battery? Could you have used cardboard strips instead?

Test the various parts of a flashlight bulb. Is the metal side of the bulb a conductor? How about the small metal knob at the bottom of the bulb?

What about the ceramic material around the metal knob? How do you know that the bulb's filament is a conductor? Can you explain now why the wires have to touch certain places to make a bulb light?

Charge must flow through the inside of a D cell, but which parts of the outside of a D cell will conduct charge? Do you think any liquids will conduct electric charge?

Procedure:

1. Place the liquid you want to test in a small plastic medicine cup or vial. Slide two paper clips over the sides of the container as shown in Figure 25c. The lower half of each clip should be submerged in liquid.

2. Touch the lead wire from the D cell to the top of one paper clip. Check to be sure that the two paper clips are not in contact, and then touch the other paper clip with the wire from the coil.

3. Test a number of different liquids such as water, milk, lemon and other juices, vinegar, carbonated soda, and solutions of salt, sugar, and baking soda.

Results and Conclusions

If the meter needle turns, what does this tell you about the liquid you are testing?

If the meter's needle does not turn, the liquid may be a nonconductor, or it may be a poor conductor. Do you see gas bubbles forming around either of the paper clips? The bubbles show that even though there is not enough electric current to turn the needle, there is enough to cause some kind of chemical reaction around the paper clips. Will the needle turn if you use a 2-D-cell battery? A 4-D-cell battery?

EXPERIMENT 4.5

Magnetic Coils

Question:
Does a current-carrying coil become magnetic?

Hypothesis:
Yes, as long as there is electricity flowing through it.

Materials:
- Two 5-m (16-ft) lengths of 24-gauge enamel-coated copper wire
- 2 D cells
- tape
- fine sandpaper
- insulated wires with alligator clips
- magnetic compass
- ruler

Once Oersted's discovery became known, scientists realized that magnets could be made by sending electric currents through coils of wire. André Ampère, a French physicist, showed that the magnetic effects produced by electricity could be used to detect and measure electric current. You have already built a coil that can detect a current. In this experiment, you will see that current-carrying coils really do behave like magnets.

Procedure:

1. Obtain two 5-m (16-ft) lengths of 24-gauge enamel-coated copper wire. (The enamel on the wire insulates it so that you can wind the wire into a coil without producing a short circuit.) Wind each length of wire into a coil by wrapping it around a D cell as shown in Figure 26a. Slide the coil of wire off the D cell.

2. Wrap small pieces of tape around the coils to hold the wires in place. Leave about 30 cm (1 ft) of wire uncoiled at each end. These straight wires will be used to connect the coil to a D cell.

3. Use fine sandpaper to remove about 3 cm (1 in) of enamel insulation from each end of each coil.

4. If you attach the two ends of the wire from a coil to a D cell as shown in Figure 26b, a current will flow through the coil. **Do not leave the coil connected longer than necessary or you will wear out the D cell!**

5. With the coil hanging from a D cell, bring a magnetic compass close to the coil. How can you tell that the coil behaves like a magnet? Which side of the coil is the north-seeking pole?

   Attach the second coil to another D cell. Does it also behave like a magnet?

Results and Conclusions

What do you think will happen if you hold the faces of these two coils close together, as shown in Figure 26c? Try it! Were you right? How can you make the coils repel one another? How can you make them attract one another?

Figure 26.

a)

b)

D cell

insulated
wires

c)

tape

a) Make two coils by winding enamel-
   coated wire around a D cell.
b) Suspend the coils from a D cell.
   Are the coils magnetic?
c) Bring two coils close together.
   What happens?

EXPERIMENT 4.6

Electromagnets

Question:

How does wrapping wire coils around an iron nail affect the magnetic field when current flows?

Hypothesis:

The iron magnifies the strength of the magnetic field many, many times.

Materials:

- 1 meter (1 yard) of enamel-coated copper wire
- iron nail
- sandpaper
- D cell
- paper clips
- insulated wires with alligator clips

Oersted's discovery of the magnetic field around moving charge led almost immediately to new technology. William Sturgeon, an English physicist, accidentally discovered that if a coil of wire were wrapped around an iron core, the strength of the magnetic field would be concentrated in the iron. He used varnish on a U-shaped piece of iron to insulate it from the metal wire. He then ran a current through the wire coil and was able to lift a 4-kg (9-lb) weight with an iron core that weighed only 0.2 kg (7 oz).

A short time later, American physicist Joseph Henry improved upon Sturgeon's design. He wrapped silk strips torn from his wife's old dresses to insulate wire he wound around an iron core. By so doing he was able to wind layer after layer of wire around the iron. In 1831, at a demonstration at Yale University, Henry lifted more than a ton of iron with what became known as an electromagnet.

Today, this technology is used to lift and move huge piles of scrap metal. First the scrap metal is lifted with an electromagnet. The scrap metal is moved. Then the current in the coil is reversed. This changes the polarity of the electromagnet. Since the magnetism that was induced in the scrap metal was of the opposite magnetic polarity, it is no longer attracted by the electromagnet and falls off. Electromagnets are also used to seal bank vaults.

Procedure:

1. To make a small electromagnet, wrap about a meter (a yard) of enamel-coated copper wire around an iron nail. Always wrap the wire in the same direction.

2. Sandpaper the ends of the wire to remove the enamel.

Figure 27.

enamel-coated
copper wire

D cell

You can make an electromagnet. How strong is it?

3. Connect the ends of the coil to a D cell, as shown in Figure 27.

How many paper clips can your electromagnet lift? (Do not connect the electromagnet to the battery for very long. The battery will wear out quickly under such conditions.)

How many paper clips can you lift with the coil if you take out the nail?

Rebuild the electromagnet, but this time wind half the turns in one direction and the other half in the opposite direction.

Results and Conclusions

Predict the number of paper clips your electromagnet will lift now. Were you right? Can you explain why?

 Science Project Ideas

- Design an experiment to show whether the number of turns in the coil affects the strength of an electromagnet.

- Can metals other than iron or steel be used as the cores for an electromagnet? Design an experiment to find out.

CHAPTER 5

Electricity, Magnets, and Motors

After Oersted discovered that magnetic fields are produced by electric currents, scientists began to look for other connections between electricity and magnetism. Within a year of Oersted's discovery, the great English scientist Michael Faraday made another scientific breakthrough. Faraday reasoned that if a current could produce a force on a magnet, a magnet should be able to produce a force on a current. In Experiment 5.1, you will perform an experiment similar to one that Faraday, in England, and Joseph Henry, in the United States, conducted to test this idea.

Faraday and Henry also reasoned that since moving charge can produce a magnetic field, a magnetic field should be able to make charges move. That is, it should be possible to use a magnetic field to induce an electric current in a wire. In Experiment 5.3, you will find, as did Faraday and Henry, the secret to using a magnetic field to induce an electric current.

◀A bar magnet attracts iron filings, which take on the form of the magnet's electric field.

EXPERIMENT 5.1

A Current in a Magnetic Field

Question:

What effect does a magnetic field have on current?

Hypothesis:

A magnetic field can put force on a current-carrying wire, making it move.

Materials:

- strong horseshoe magnet or 4 to 6 ceramic magnets
- bare copper wire
- D cell
- insulated wires with alligator clips
- tape

You have seen that a magnetic field surrounds an electric current. When charges move, a magnetic field is created. Will a magnetic field have any effect on an electric current? You might think so. After all, an electric current is surrounded by a magnetic field, and magnetic fields can attract or repel one another.

To find out, you can use either a strong horseshoe magnet or four to six ceramic magnets.

Procedure:

1. If you use a horseshoe magnet, suspend a swing-shaped piece of bare copper wire from a D cell as shown in Figure 28a. Use insulated wires to connect the copper wire to the D cell. Be sure the suspended copper wire can swing freely.

a)

D cell

flexible insulated wires

copper wire "swing"

strong horseshoe magnet

N

S

Figure 28.

To see the effect of a magnetic field on a current, let a current flow in a direction perpendicular to a magnetic field.

b)

D cell

flexible, insulated wire

ceramic magnets

tape

tape

2. Bring the short side of the copper wire between the poles of the magnet as shown. Then connect the wire to a D cell so that a current flows through the copper wire in the magnetic field. The wire will be pushed either into or out of the magnet. Which way is it pushed? What happens to the direction the wire is pushed if you turn the D cell around?

3. If you use ceramic magnets, place four or six of the magnets so that they are attracted to each other and form a column. Divide the group of magnets in the middle so that you have two groups of magnets. The two groups will attract one another.

4. Separate the two groups by 1 cm (0.5 in) and tape them down that far apart.

5. Use a long, flexible, insulated wire to make a loop as shown in Figure 28b. The ends of the wire should be bare. Place the loop—the center of the wire—between the faces of the magnets. Tape the wire in place as shown. Be sure the loop between the magnets can move up or down easily.

6. Touch the bare ends of the wire to the opposite poles of a D cell.

Results and Conclusions

Notice that the loop of wire between the faces of the magnets is pushed either up or down. Which way is it pushed? What happens to the direction the wire is pushed if you turn the D cell around? How might this basic principle be used to build an electric motor?

 ## Science Project Idea

- Design and carry out an experiment to measure the force exerted on a current by a magnetic field. Does the size of the force depend on the current? Does the size of the force depend on the strength of the magnetic field?

Electric Motors

Faraday discovered that there is a force on a current-carrying wire when the current runs across a magnetic field. He realized that such a force could be used to make a motor that would do work. He demonstrated that possibility by building the simple motor shown in Figure 29.

Figure 29.

In Faraday's electric motor, a magnet rotated around a fixed wire (left), and a wire rotated around a fixed magnet (right). A battery provided current, and mercury allowed current to reach both the fixed and the rotating wires.

Today, electric motors are everywhere, and, in increasing numbers, they are found in automobiles. Gasoline-powered cars contribute to air pollution and produce greenhouse gases, such as carbon dioxide, that cause global warming. Electric cars powered by fuel cells do not. Replacing gasoline-powered cars with electric cars would reduce pollution and greenhouse gases significantly.

A variety of electric cars are on the market or being developed. All of them have an efficient motor that turns the car's wheels and obtains and stores energy when the car slows down. The energy obtained during slowdowns (braking) returns as much as half of the car's kinetic (motion) energy to batteries or fuel cells. Furthermore, unlike an internal combustion engine, the electric motor requires no energy when at rest or coasting.

A gasoline engine makes use of less than one fourth of the energy in the fuel it burns. On the other hand, an electric motor can change more than 90 percent of the potential energy stored in the chemicals of the battery that drive it into kinetic energy. Electric cars powered by hydrogen fuel cells release only water as an end product. Gone are the carbon monoxide and carbon dioxide gases that contribute to pollution and global warming.

Increasingly popular are hybrid cars. These cars are powered by an electric motor combined with a small internal combustion engine. The internal combustion engine is used to charge batteries or fuel cells when necessary. The drawback to electric or hybrid cars is their initial cost. However, fuel costs are considerably less, and electric motors have a longer life span. When the health and economic costs related to pollution and global warming are considered, electric cars are very competitive.

EXPERIMENT 5.2

A Current in a Magnetic Field and Motors

Question:

What basic principle makes electric motors work?

Hypothesis:

Electric motors operate because of the force exerted by a magnet on an electric current.

Materials:

- **an adult**
- Styrofoam cup
- 2 large paper clips
- tape
- 3 ceramic magnets
- 30-cm (1-ft) length of enamel-coated copper wire
- sandpaper
- insulated wires with alligator clips
- 4-D-cell battery or 6-volt dry cell battery
- pliers
- plastic darning or thin knitting needle
- wine cork
- sharp knife
- about 8 m (25 ft) of thin enamel-coated copper wire
- pins

continued

continued

- tin snips
- tin can
- hammer
- small nail
- 3 tacks or small screws
- wood block about 15 cm x 15 cm x 2.5 cm (6 in x 6 in x 1 in)

- two 30-cm (1-ft) pieces of insulated copper wire
- thumbtacks
- strong horseshoe magnet or 6 to 8 ceramic magnets

You have seen that a magnetic field surrounds an electric current. When charges move, a magnetic field is created. In the previous experiment, you saw that a magnetic field can push on a wire carrying an electric current. Electric motors are based on the principle that a magnetic field will exert a force on a current-carrying wire.

Michael Faraday built the world's first electric motor. It was more a toy than a practical machine. But it was based on the interaction between electric currents and magnets—a new science developed by Faraday, Henry, Oersted, Ampère, and others.

You can apply this principle by building a very simple electric motor.

Procedure:

1. Make a stand for your motor by inverting a Styrofoam cup. Then unfold one end of each of two large paper clips. Tape them to opposite sides of the cup, as shown in Figure 30.

Figure 30.

You can build a simple DC motor.

2. Place two disk or rectangular ceramic magnets on top of the inverted cup. Place a third magnet inside the cup and directly beneath the other two. This procedure will add strength to the magnet and help to hold it in place.

3. The coil, which forms the turning part of the motor, can be made by winding about 30 cm (1 ft) of enamel-coated copper wire three or four times around your first two fingers. Leave some extra wire on each end.

4. Take the coil off your fingers. Wrap the ends around opposite sides of the coil several times to help keep the coil wires in place. Two tiny pieces of tape can be used to hold the wires of the coil in place as shown. The unwrapped end pieces should be about 5 cm (2 in) long. Straighten and then sandpaper these ends to remove the enamel.

5. The sandpapered ends of the coil fit into the loops you made with the paper clips. Turn the coil gently. It should come very close to the top of the magnet. If necessary, adjust the position of the paper clip supports.

6. Use wires with alligator clips on each end to connect the poles of a 4-D-cell battery or a 6-volt dry cell to the paper clips that support the coil of the motor. Give the coil a gentle flip and watch it spin.

Results and Conclusions

Actually, this motor should not work. Motors that are operated by a battery (DC motors) have a commutator—a device that stops the current in the coil every half turn. Without the commutator, such motors would make only half a turn. Then the force of the magnetic field on the current that you saw in Experiment 5.1 would simply stretch the coil; the coil would not turn any longer.

In the simple motor you made, the coil is so light that it bounces on the paper clip loops and breaks the electrical connection, allowing the coil to rotate past the point where it would simply be stretched.

Following are instructions for how you can make a more complicated electric motor.

Procedure:

1. **Ask an adult** to use pliers to force a plastic darning or thin knitting needle through the center of a wine cork. **Ask the adult** to also use a sharp knife to cut a V-shaped notch along the sides of the cork.

2. You can then wind 70 turns of thin enamel-coated copper wire around the cork using the notches to support the wire. You have just made what is called the motor's rotor.

3. Use sandpaper to remove the enamel insulation from about 3 cm (1 in) of each end of the wire coil you have made. Insert a common pin on each side of the coil as shown in Figure 31a. Firmly wind one bared end of wire around one pin and the other bared end around the other pin. The pins and their connections to the rotor make up the commutator, an essential part of a DC motor.

4. Next, build a support for the rotor. **Ask an adult** to cut two strips from a tin can, each 2-cm- (¾-in-) wide. The strips should be about twice as long as the cork. Use a hammer and a small nail to punch three holes through one end of each strip. These holes will be used to attach the strip to a wood block, as shown in Figure 31b. Punch another hole through the center of each strip about 4 cm (1.5 in) above the nearest of the three holes you punched before. These holes will support the ends of the darning or knitting needle. Use three tacks or small screws to fix each metal strip to the block of wood.

5. Using pliers, bend the upper ends of each strip into a semicircle as shown.

6. Insert the darning or knitting needle of the rotor through the upper holes in the metal strips. Make sure the rotor turns easily. If it does not, you will have to enlarge the holes.

7. Make the brushes from two 30-cm (1-ft) pieces of insulated copper wire. Remove about 5 cm (2 in) of insulation from both ends of each wire.

8. Using thumbtacks, fasten each wire to the wooden block so that a bare end of each wire rubs against a commutator pin. Later, you will connect the other ends of the two wires to a 6-volt (4-D-cell) battery.

9. Put a strong horseshoe magnet in position as shown in Figure 31c. If you do not have such a magnet, you can use ceramic magnets on either side of the coil. Of course, opposite poles of the two magnets should face each other to produce a strong field across the coil. Give the coil a flip and your motor should spin if all connections make contact.

Figure 31.

a) cork, pins, needle, insulated (enameled) wire, bare wire

b) wood block, tacks or screws

c) insulated wire, large horseshoe magnet, brushes, thumbtack

You can build a DC motor with a commutator from simple materials.

Results and Conclusions

Watch to see which way the motor turns. If you reverse the connections to the battery, does the motor reverse the direction it turns? What happens to the direction the motor turns if you reverse the poles of the magnet?

 Science Project Idea

- To understand how important Faraday's discovery was, make a list of all the devices you can think of that use electric motors.

Electric Currents From Magnets

Faraday, like most scientists, believed that nature was uniform. Therefore, since an electric current produces a magnetic field, he reasoned a magnetic field should be able to produce an electric current. To test his hypothesis, Faraday placed very strong magnets near and around coils of wire. But nothing happened. There were no electric currents in the coils. He used bigger magnets and more coils of wire; still nothing. Then, on Christmas Day in 1831, Faraday discovered the key to producing a current from magnets. He wrapped a coil of wire around part of an iron ring and connected the coil to a battery. On the other side of the ring, he wrapped another coil of wire and connected it to a meter. When he closed the switch between the battery and the coil, his electric meter revealed that charges flowed, and a momentary current was produced in the other coil. When he opened the switch, the needle moved again, but in the opposite direction.

When he saw the meter's needle move, first one way and then the other, Faraday realized what was needed to generate an electric current from magnets. A steady magnetic field, no matter how big, had no effect on electric charges. What was necessary was a changing magnetic field. Oersted had shown that electric charges must be *moving* to produce a magnetic field. Faraday discovered that a magnetic field had to be *changing* to make electric charges move.

Faraday pictured a magnetic field as lines of force, like those in the pattern made by the iron filings in Experiment 3.2, Figure 20b. He imagined a strong field to consist of many closely packed lines of force. A weak field he thought of as fewer lines less closely packed. Whenever the number of field lines through a coil of wire increased or decreased, electric charges were forced to move. Or, if a wire moved across magnetic field lines, there was a force on charges in the wire.

EXPERIMENT 5.3

A Current From a Magnetic Field

Question:

What is the most important use of Faraday's discovery regarding magnets and electric current?

Hypothesis:

Faraday's discovery led to the creation of electromagnetic generators that create electricity.

Materials:

- the meter you built in Experiment 4.3
- a coil made from 10 m (33 ft) of 24-gauge insulated wire and the core of a roll of duct tape
- 2 long insulated wires
- strong bar magnet or about 12 ceramic magnets
- a partner
- strong horseshoe magnet (optional)

A generator based on the principle that Faraday discovered and one that you can build is shown in Figure 32. It consists of two coils, one of which is the meter you built in Experiment 4.3.

Procedure:

1. You will need to build a second identical coil without the compass needle. The second coil should be far enough away from the meter that a magnet has no effect on the meter. You will also need two long insulated wires to connect the ends of the two coils.

2. You can change the magnetic field through the second or unmetered coil by moving a magnet in and out of the coil. You can use either a strong bar magnet or about six or more ceramic magnets that are joined together.

Figure 32.

You can make a simple generator.

Results and Conclusions

What happens to the meter's needle as you move the magnet in and out of the coil? Which way does the compass needle turn when the south-seeking pole of the magnet is pushed into the coil? Which way does it turn when the magnet is pulled out of the coil? Which way does the compass needle turn when the north-seeking pole is pushed into the coil? Which way does it turn when the magnet is pulled out of the coil?

To change the rate at which the magnetic field changes, you can move the magnet at different speeds. Does the rate at which the magnetic field changes affect the current that is induced?

Is there any effect if you do not move the magnet? Can you generate a current by moving the coil while a partner holds the magnet? Is the induced current affected by the number of turns of wire in the coil? Conduct an experiment to find out.

In Experiment 5.1, you saw that electric charges moving in a wire perpendicular to a magnetic field are pushed in a direction perpendicular to both the field and the current. You might suspect that if you pulled electric charges across a magnetic field there would be a force on those charges. If that force were parallel to the wire, charges within the wire would be forced along it, creating an electric current. Here is how to test that idea.

Procedure:

1. Connect the unmetered coil to the electric meter with long insulated wires. Be sure the second coil is far enough from the meter that a magnet has no effect on the meter.

2. If you have a large, strong horseshoe magnet, you can pull the coil across the magnetic field as shown in Figure 33a. If you do not have such a magnet, you can use a stack of about a dozen ceramic magnets. Separate the magnets at their center.

3. Have a partner hold the two attracting magnets apart at a distance slightly larger than the width of the coil. Move the coil quickly through the magnetic field as shown in Figure 33b.

Figure 33.

a)

b)

Does pulling the charges in a wire across a magnetic field cause them to move, creating an electric current? You can find out by using
a) a coil and a strong horseshoe magnet, or
b) a coil and ceramic magnets held in place by a partner.

Results and Conclusions

Regardless of the magnet you use, what happens as the wires in the coil move across a magnetic field? Is a current induced in the wire? Does pushing the coil into the field have a different effect than pulling the coil out of the field? If it does, can you explain why?

 Science Project Idea

- Design and build an electric generator strong enough to light a flashlight bulb.

Figure 34.

wires to telegraph

zinc
sulfate
solution

zinc
electrode

copper
sulfate
solution

copper
electrode

The drawing shows a Daniell cell. It can
supply a steady current for a long time.

CHAPTER 6

Electricity and Chemistry

When the telegraph was first used to send messages by wire, a steady source of current was needed. The solution was the Daniell cell, which had been invented in 1836 by an English chemist, John Daniell. A drawing of a Daniell cell is shown in Figure 34. It consists of a large jar, solutions, and electrodes (materials that conduct electrical current into or out of an electrolyte). A solution of a blue compound, copper sulfate, occupies the lower half of the jar. It surrounds a fanlike copper electrode.

A less dense solution of zinc sulfate lies above the copper sulfate solution. Suspended inside the zinc sulfate solution is a heavy three-pronged zinc electrode, which was often referred to as a crow's foot. The zinc electrode was large because during the chemical reaction that produced an electric current, the zinc dissolved. At the same time, copper collected (plated) on the copper electrode. As zinc atoms dissolved, they released negative charges (electrons). The electrons flowed through the circuit containing the telegraph and back to the copper electrode at the bottom of the cell. There, copper ions (positively charged atoms) in the solution combined with the electrons and plated onto the copper electrode as copper atoms. Because zinc releases negative charges, the zinc is the Daniell cell's negative electrode; the copper is the positive electrode.

You will have an opportunity to see how a Daniell cell works in Experiment 6.1. And, in Experiment 6.2, you will look inside a D cell.

EXPERIMENT 6.1

Inside a Daniell Cell

Question:
How do chemical reactions generate electricity?

Hypothesis:
A chemical reaction causes the release and the acceptance of ions and electrons—an electric current.

Materials:
- **an adult**
- safety goggles
- zinc sulfate ($ZnSO_4 \cdot 7\ H_2O$)
- metric scale
- spoon
- two 1-L flasks
- water
- baby food jars
- paper towel
- strips of copper and zinc 4 cm x 1 cm (1.6 in x 0.4 in)
- copper sulfate ($CuSO_4 \cdot 5H_2O$)
- insulated wires
- galvanometer or electric meter from Experiment 4.3

In this experiment you will be working with chemicals. Be sure to **wear safety goggles and work under adult supervision**. Also, be sure to **wash your hands thoroughly afterward.** It will help you to keep written notes of the many quick experiments you will be doing with chemicals.

To keep a Daniell cell working for long periods of time, it was essential that the solutions and electrodes be kept apart. Even though the solutions were in contact, there was very little mixing. The copper sulfate was denser than the zinc sulfate, so it tended to remain at the bottom of the jar. Furthermore, when the cell was providing a current, copper ions kept moving toward the copper electrode.

You will use copper sulfate and zinc sulfate solutions in these experiments.

Procedure:

1. To prepare the zinc sulfate solution, add 25 g of zinc sulfate (ZnSO$_4$ · 7 H$_2$O) to 1 liter of water and stir. To prepare the copper sulfate solution, add 25 g of copper sulfate (CuSO$_4$ · 5 H$_2$O) to 1 liter of water and stir.

2. To see why the solutions and electrodes in the Daniell cell were kept apart, dip a strip of copper into a baby food jar that contains some copper sulfate solution. Leave it for about a minute. Then remove it. Did anything happen to the copper strip?

3. Rinse the copper strip in water. Then dip it in some zinc sulfate solution for a minute. Did anything happen? What would happen if zinc sulfate solution reached the copper electrode?

   Is there any noticeable reaction if you place a zinc strip in a zinc sulfate solution?

4. Rinse the zinc strip in water. Then place it in copper sulfate solution for a minute. What do you observe? What happens if you leave the copper in the zinc sulfate for several minutes? If you leave it overnight? What would eventually happen to the zinc electrode in a Daniell cell if it were in contact with copper sulfate?

5. Use insulated wires to connect two zinc strips to your electric meter or to a galvanometer. Dip both strips into a baby food jar containing zinc sulfate solution as shown in Figure 35. Is any current produced?

Figure 35.

Will zinc strips in zinc sulfate produce a current? How about copper strips in copper sulfate? How about one copper strip in copper sulfate and one zinc strip in zinc sulfate?

6. After rinsing the zinc strips, dip them both into a solution of copper sulfate solution. Is there any current?

7. Next, connect two copper strips to your electric meter or to a galvanometer. Dip both strips into a baby food jar containing zinc sulfate solution. Is any current produced? After rinsing the copper strips, dip them both into a solution of copper sulfate solution. Is there any current?

8. Now connect a zinc strip and a copper strip to the galvanometer or to your electric meter. Is there a current when you dip these strips into zinc sulfate? Is there a current when you dip these strips into copper sulfate?

9. Finally, connect a zinc strip and a copper strip to the galvanometer or to your electric meter. Place the zinc strip in a solution of zinc sulfate. In a separate jar, place the copper strip in a copper sulfate solution. Is there any current? Now connect the two solutions with a paper towel strip as shown in Figure 36.

Results and Conclusions

What happens when the two solutions diffuse along the towel and meet?

 Science Project Idea

- Your science teacher may be able to help you obtain a Daniell cell. Figure out a way to place the copper sulfate solution below the zinc sulfate solution without mixing them. Connect the cell to a low-wattage bulb in series with an ammeter. What current flows? For how long will the cell provide current for the lightbulb?

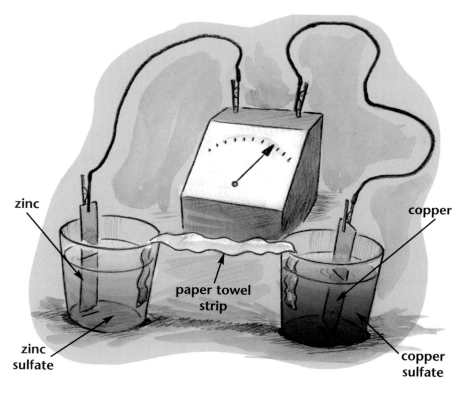

zinc

copper

paper towel
strip

zinc
sulfate

copper
sulfate

Figure 36.

What is the purpose of the paper towel? Will there be a current without it?

EXPERIMENT 6.2

Inside a D cell

Question:
Why are D-cell batteries termed "dry cells"?

Hypothesis:
D cells use a powder electrolyte rather than a liquid electrolyte.

Materials:
- **an adult**
- D cell
- hacksaw
- electric meter from Experiment 4.3

A Daniell cell, like all electric cells, has two electrodes and an electrolyte. The electrolyte is a liquid or a damp solid through which charges can move. As you saw in Experiment 6.1, charges must be able to flow within the cell as well as outside. The electrolyte makes this possible. When the copper sulfate and zinc sulfate solutions were separated, no current could flow. Connecting them with a wet paper towel provided a bridge through which charges could move from one electrode to the other.

Ordinary D cells, which are used in flashlights, are quite different than Daniell cells.

Procedure:

1. To see what is inside a D cell, **ask an adult** to use a hacksaw to cut a D cell in half lengthwise, as shown in Figure 37. The black rod extending through the center of the cell is the positive electrode. The zinc can, which is insulated from the carbon rod, is the negative electrode, just as it was in the Daniell cell. The electrolyte is a moist black mixture of carbon powder, manganese dioxide, and ammonium chloride. The porous separator allows ammonium chloride to reach the zinc can but prevents manganese dioxide and carbon from making contact with the zinc.

2. Using the ends of the two wires from the electric meter you made in Experiment 4.3, touch the carbon rod in two different places.

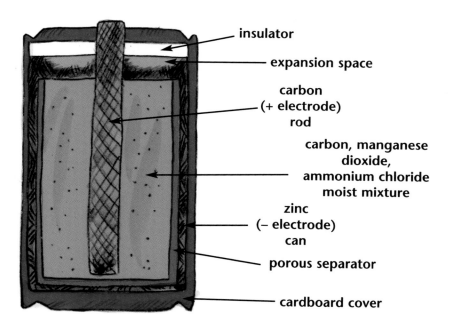

insulator

expansion space

carbon
(+ electrode)
rod

carbon, manganese
dioxide,
ammonium chloride
moist mixture

zinc
(– electrode)
can

porous separator

cardboard cover

Figure 37.

The diagram shows a D cell cut in half. Not all D cells have a cardboard cover. A carbon rod is the positive electrode. The zinc can is the negative electrode. A moist mixture of carbon, manganese dioxide, and ammonium chloride serves as the electrolyte.

Results and Conclusions

Does a current flow when you do this? Does a current flow when you touch the carbon rod and the zinc can? Will there be a current if you touch the zinc can and the black electrolyte? How about if you touch the carbon rod and the electrolyte?

Why do you think D cells are often called dry cells?

 Science Project Ideas

- Which parts of the D cell do you think will conduct an electric current? Design an experiment to find out.

- Some people keep electric cells, such as D cells, in their refrigerator. Do D cells have a longer shelf life if kept cool? Design an experiment to find out.

EXPERIMENT 6.3

The Minimum Ingredients for an Electric Cell

Question:

What are the essential components of an electric cell?

Hypothesis:

To produce electricity, the cell needs two different types of electrodes and an electrolyte.

Materials:

- zinc and copper strips
- an olive
- insulated wires
- a lemon
- galvanometer and/or microammeter
- copper, aluminum, and steel nails
- electric meter from Experiment 4.3
- various fruits
- steel wool
- 3 copper pennies
- 3 steel washers
- blotter paper
- scissors
- salt
- water
- cup
- clothespins

As you have seen, an electric cell needs two different electrodes and an electrolyte. Even nails or strips of two different metals stuck in a piece of fruit can act as an electric cell. This experiment demonstrates that this is true.

Procedure:

1. Push a zinc strip and a copper strip into an olive. Be sure the strips are close together.

2. Use insulated wires to connect the metal strips to the electric meter you built in Experiment 4.3 or to a galvanometer. Does a current flow?

3. Repeat the experiment using a lemon. If you do not obtain a current, try squeezing the lemon to break up the internal sections. If you still cannot detect a current, connect the electrodes to a galvanometer or to a microammeter, which measures millionths of an ampere.

Results and Conclusions

If placed in an olive, will a copper and an aluminum nail produce a current? A steel and a copper nail? A steel and an aluminum nail? How about two copper nails?

Can other fruits also serve as electrolytes? Design experiments to find out.

The First Electric Cell

Luigi Galvani was an eighteenth-century Italian scientist who taught anatomy to medical students. Galvani discovered that if he touched a frog's leg with two different metals, the leg would twitch. Galvani thought that the electricity came from the frog. Another eighteenth-century Italian scientist, Alessandro Volta, thought the electricity involved the interaction of the two different metals.

To show that the electricity came from the two different metals, Volta built a battery. He placed disks of copper and zinc alternately in a stack with cardboard soaked in salt water between them. Volta had made the world's first battery, which produced a direct current.

You can make a simple battery like Volta's.

Procedure:

1. Use steel wool to polish three copper pennies and three steel washers so that they are shiny.

2. Cut blotter paper into circles that are slightly larger than the pennies and washers. Soak the paper circles in a concentrated solution of salt and water.

3. Make a paper "sandwich" by placing the wet paper between a penny and a washer as shown in Figure 38a. Hold the sandwich together with a clothespin.

4. Touch the ends of the wires from your electric meter to the electric cell as shown. Does the meter indicate a current? If not, make the stack larger by adding in alternate fashion penny, wet paper, steel washer until you have a 3-cell battery as shown in Figure 38b.

5. Test this battery with your electric meter.

Figure 38.

a) clothespin

steel washer

penny

blotter paper soaked in salt water

to electric meter

b)

pennies

steel washers

a) Make an electric cell from a penny, a steel washer, and a blotter-paper disk soaked in salt solution. Test this cell with your electric meter.
b) Make a battery by stacking three cells together.

Results and Conclusions

Is the current detectable? If not, try testing with a galvanometer or a microammeter. What are the electrodes in this simple battery? What is the electrolyte?

 Science Project Ideas

- You may have seen science books that show a flashlight bulb being lighted by a lemon. Is this possible? Design an experiment to find out.

- Investigate the corrosion of metals. How is corrosion related to electric cells?

- Build the electrical instrument that was named for Galvani.

- Build the electrical meter that was named for Volta and explain how it works.

By now you have seen that electric charges can be at rest, as they are in a cloud. Or they can be moving, as they are when an electric current flows. The world's largest electric currents occur when the attraction between static charges of opposite sign (+ and −) in clouds or between clouds and the ground becomes so large that the charges flow through the air. We call this huge current lightning.

More useful and far less dangerous currents are produced by the batteries and generators you have investigated. These currents are used to light our homes, schools, and industries; turn our many electric motors; and run our electronic devices such as computers.

The similarity between electricity and magnetism, which for many centuries could not be explained, is no longer a mystery to you. You have seen how magnetic fields arise from electric currents and how changing magnetic fields can induce electric currents. Along the way, you have learned how to build simple switches, electric meters and motors, electromagnets, electric cells, as well as how to plate metals and send messages using electricity.

Many of the mysteries about electricity and magnetism are no longer so mysterious. Your experiments have answered many questions. But there is much more to learn. What you have discovered here may inspire you to continue with further study of the fascinating subject of electricity and magnetism.

Appendix
SCIENCE SUPPLY COMPANIES

Carolina Biological Supply Company
2700 York Road
Burlington, NC 27215-3398
(800) 334-5551
http://www.carolina.com

Connecticut Valley Biological
   Supply Company
82 Valley Road
P.O. Box 326
Southampton, MA 01073
(800) 628-7748
http://www.ctvalleybio.com

Delta Education
80 Northwest Boulevard
P.O. Box 3000
Nashua, NH 03061-3000
(800) 258-1302
http://www.delta-education.com

Edmund Scientifics
60 Pearce Avenue
Tonawanda, NY 14150-6711
(800) 728-6999
http://scientificsonline.com

Educational Innovations, Inc.
362 Main Avenue
Norwalk, CT 06851
(888) 912-7474
http://www.teachersource.com

Fisher Science Education
4500 Turnberry Drive
Hanover Park, IL 60133
(800) 955-1177
http://www.fisheredu.com

Frey Scientific
80 Northwest Boulevard
Nashua, NH 03063
(800) 225-3739
http://www.freyscientific.com/

NASCO-Fort Atkinson
901 Janesville Avenue
P.O. Box 901
Fort Atkinson, WI 53538-0901
(800) 558-9595
http://www.nascofa.com/

NASCO-Modesto
4825 Stoddard Road
P.O. Box 3837
Modesto, CA 95352-3837
(800) 558-9595
http://www.enasco.com

Sargent-Welch
P.O. Box 4130
Buffalo, NY 14217
(800) 727-4368
http://www.sargentwelch.com

Science Kit & Boreal Laboratories
777 East Park Drive
P.O. Box 5003
Tonawanda, NY 14151-5003
(800) 828-7777
http://sciencekit.com

Ward's Natural Science
P.O. Box 92912
Rochester, NY 14692-9012
(800) 962-2660
http://www.wardsci.com

Further Reading

Bochinski, Julianne Blair. *The Complete Workbook for Science Fair Projects*. Hoboken, N.J.: Wiley, 2005.

DiSpezio, Michael A., Rob Collinet (Illustrator). *Awesome Experiments in Electricity & Magnetism*. New York: Sterling Pub. Co., 2006.

Green, Dan. *Physics*. New York: Kingfisher, 2008.

Haduch, Bill. *Science Fair Success Secrets: How to Win Prizes, Have Fun, and Think Like a Scientist*. New York: Dutton Children's Books, 2002.

Vecchione, Glen. *Blue Ribbon Science Projects*. New York: Sterling Pub. Co., 2005.

Other books by Robert Gardner:

Gardner, Robert. *Easy Genius Science Projects with Electricity and Magnetism*. Berkeley Heights, N.J.: Enslow Publishers, Inc., 2009.

Gardner, Robert, Madeline Goodstein, and Thomas R. Rybolt. *Ace Your Physical Science Project: Great Science Fair Ideas*. Berkeley Heights, N.J.: Enslow Publishers, Inc., 2010.

Internet Addresses

All Science Fair Projects
  <http://www.all-science-fair-projects.com/>

Exploratorium
  <http://www.exploratorium.edu/>

TryScience. "Experiments."
  <http://www.tryscience.org/experiments/experiments_
  home.html/>

Index